Good Food Made Simple

HEALTHY

Good Food Made Simple

HEALTHY

*Over 140 delicious recipes, 500 color photographs,
step-by-step images, and nutritional information*

First published in 2013
LOVE FOOD is an imprint of Parragon Books Ltd

Parragon Inc.
440 Park Avenue South, 13th Floor
New York, NY 10016

www.parragon.com/lovefood

ISBN: 978-1-4723-1917-3
Printed in China

New photography by Noel Murphy
New recipes by Christine France
New introduction and note text by Judith Wills
Edited by Lin Thomas
Nutritional analysis by Fiona Hunter

Notes for the Reader
This book uses standard kitchen measuring spoons and cups. All spoon and cup
measurements are level unless otherwise indicated. Unless otherwise stated, milk
is assumed to be whole, butter is assumed to be salted, eggs are large, individual
vegetables are medium, and pepper is freshly ground black pepper. Unless
otherwise stated, all root vegetables should be washed and peeled before using.

For the best results, use a meat thermometer when cooking meat and poultry—
check the latest USDA government guidelines for current advice.

Garnishes and serving suggestions are all optional and not necessarily included
in the recipe ingredients or method. The times given are only an approximate
guide. Preparation times differ according to the techniques used by different
people and the cooking times may also vary from those given. Optional
ingredients, variations, or serving suggestions have not been included in
the calculations.

Recipes using raw or very lightly cooked eggs should be avoided by infants,
the elderly, pregnant women, and people with weakened immune systems.
Pregnant and breast-feeding women are advised to avoid eating peanuts
and peanut products. People with nut allergies should be aware that some
of the prepared ingredients used in the recipes in this book may contain nuts.
Always check the packaging before use.

Picture acknowledgments
The publisher would like to thank the following for permission to reproduce
copyright material on page 8: Single pea on white plate © amana productions
inc./Getty Images and Five food groups © Maximilian Stock Ltd./Getty Images.

Contents

What is a balanced diet?

Most of us have heard the phrase "a balanced diet" before, but it is not always easy to know exactly what this means. What should we be eating on a daily or weekly basis? Below, we will explain what a balanced diet is and what you should be eating regularly to maintain a healthy lifestyle.

A balanced diet means eating a wide variety of foods in the right proportions. It also means consuming adequate calories from what you eat and drink so that you maintain a reasonable weight.

If we can balance the major calorie-providing nutrients, such as carbohydrates, fats, and protein, then they should provide all of the other smaller elements of a healthy diet without us having to worry too much about them. These smaller elements are called the "micronutrients"—otherwise known as vitamins, minerals, and plant chemical compounds, as well as dietary fiber.

What's on the plate?

The healthy food plate below shows the ideal proportions of food to eat each day (for an average adult).

A balanced diet means eating a wide variety of foods in the right proportions.

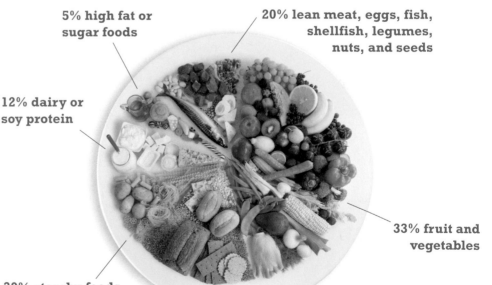

5% high fat or sugar foods

20% lean meat, eggs, fish, shellfish, legumes, nuts, and seeds

12% dairy or soy protein

33% fruit and vegetables

30% starchy foods

33 percent fruit and vegetables: These are the richest providers of many vitamins, plant chemicals, and fiber. At least five portions every day are preferable and the ideal balance is two fruits and three vegetables. Choose a rainbow of different colors to be sure you get a complete range of nutrients.

30 percent starchy foods: Starchy foods, such as grains (preferably whole), bread, pasta, and root vegetables provide a range of vitamins, minerals, plant chemicals, and fiber, as well as the calories we need.

20 percent lean meat, eggs, fish, shellfish, legumes (dried beans), nuts, and seeds: Vary your choices within this section; it is good to eat fish regularly (including oily fish), but also have meals that include legumes, such as beans or lentils, or nuts and seeds.

12 percent dairy or soy protein: This section includes milk, cheese, and yogurt, or calcium-fortified soy milk and yogurts. Cream and cream cheeses aren't included because they contain little protein and a lot of saturated fat.

5 percent high fat or high sugar foods: These are what might be called "junk foods" and should be eaten in small amounts (or not at all, if possible). This section includes sugar, sugary drinks, cakes, cookies, pastries, and confectionery.

Your recommended amounts

Nutritional experts have established some recommended levels for all of the major and micronutrients that make up a balanced diet. These include the nutrients that we need to get in adequate amounts, such as protein, certain fats, and carbohydrates, but also maximum levels for those items that we should limit, such as saturated fats, sugar, and salt. No more than 25–35 percent of your calories should come from total total, and less than 10 percent of your calories should come from saturated fat. The chart below provides some guidelines. The amount of calories you need to consume changes with age, but also with levels of physical activity.

Your healthy diet and food labeling

Nowadays, almost all manufactured food has nutritional information on the label, with the amount of each nutrient per portion usually listed. It also details the percentage of the recommended amount of each nutrient that a portion provides. Keeping an eye on labels is a good way to make sure you stay within healthy limits.

However, nutritional guidelines are there as just that—a guide to what, on average, you should be getting in your diet every day. There is no need to worry about reaching the exact figures for each nutrient each day—as long as, over the course of a week, you get a good balance.

This relaxed way of planning your diet means that you can have the occasional treat or day when you want to eat more. Don't feel guilty—all you do is cut back a little on the other days of the week. Food gives you life and health but don't forget, it is also there to be enjoyed—within reasonable limits.

Our recommended daily amounts*

	Cal	Fat	Sat Fat**	Carbs	Sugar**	Protein***	Fiber***	Salt**
Men	2,600	95g	30g	130g	120g	55g	38g	6g
Women	2,000	76g	20g	130g	90g	45g	25g	6g

* Based on the average adult male and female—individuals may need more or less.

** Recommended maximum—less is probably preferable.

*** Recommended minimum—more may be preferable.

What is healthy food?

A healthy food is one that contains a good level and variety of nutrients, as well as being low in components known to have an adverse effect on us. Most experts also say that a healthy diet is one that contains a high proportion of unprocessed, or minimally processed, natural foods, especially plant foods.

Most experts say that a healthy diet is one that contains a high proportion of unprocessed, natural foods.

Some of the most important nutrients for health are those that we need only in small amounts, but are essential for good health. These are vitamins, minerals, essential fatty acids, and a vast range of plant chemicals, which are the newest stars of the nutrition world.

Vitamins

Vitamins are minute particles that help to protect us from disease and are important in the day-to-day functioning, protection, and maintenance of our bodies.

Vitamins that we need regularly but not necessarily every day because they can be stored in the body are:

Vitamin A—for healthy growth, skin, and vision, found mainly in meat, dairy produce, and eggs. The body can also convert carotenes, found in brightly colored plant foods, into vitamin A.

Vitamin D—for calcium absorption and other functions, found in oily fish and eggs.

Vitamin E—a powerful antioxidant that helps prevent heart disease, found in nuts, seeds, other plant oils, and some other plant foods.

Vitamin K—for normal blood clotting, found in a wide variety of foods.

Vitamins we need daily, ideally, because they cannot be stored in the body are:

Vitamin C—for the immune system, to help iron absorption, and many other roles, such as being an antioxidant. Found in fruit and vegetables.

Vitamin B group—these work together for growth, a healthy nervous system, and food metabolism. Found in meat, fish, legumes, eggs, and dairy produce.

Minerals

There are 15 minerals that we need to get from what we eat and drink. The major minerals that we often lack enough of are:

Calcium—for healthy bones and with several other roles, found in dairy produce, nuts, seeds, and dried fruit.

Iron—for healthy blood and transportation of oxygen, found in meat, legumes, whole grains, and leafy greens.

Magnesium—for bone density, and a healthy nervous system, heart, and muscles, found in nuts, seeds, and dairy produce.

Potassium—for regulating blood pressure and for a healthy heart, found in many fruits and vegetables.

Zinc—for a healthy immune system, skin, and fertility, found in red meat, shellfish, nuts, and seeds.

Selenium—for a healthy immune system, found in nuts, legumes, and fish.

Fats in your diet

All fats—at 9 calories per gram— are a concentrated source of energy, but the types of fat we find in our food and their effects on our health can vary considerably.

Saturated fats—These are the solid fats found in highest amounts in animals fats, such as lard, butter, fatty meats, and high-fat dairy produce. Overconsumption is linked with increased blood cholesterol and heart disease.

Trans fats—These occur naturally in foods, such as meat and high-fat dairy produce, but can also occur in processed foods, such as cookies and cakes. They can raise blood cholesterol and are linked to increased risk of heart disease.

Monounsaturated fats—These are found in certain plant foods and their oils, including olive oil, avocados, canola oil, and hazelnuts. Regular consumption appears to have a protective effect against both heart disease and some types of cancer.

Polyunsaturated fats—These are found in a range of plant foods, such as corn oil, sunflower oil, safflower oil, blended vegetable oil, nuts, seeds, and processed soft margarines. While this group contains the "essential fatty acids" (see below) and can help lower blood cholesterol, our intake of polyunsaturated fats tends to be more than adequate.

Essential fatty acids—Within the polyunsaturated group of fats there are two essential fats that the body can't manufacture itself: the omega-6 fat linoleic acid (found in nuts and seeds and their oils) and the omega-3 fat alpha-linolenic acid or ALA (found in flaxseed, flaxseed oil, canola oil, and walnut oil). The body can convert ALA to

EPA and DHA—two omega-3 fatty acids linked with protection from heart disease and with a variety of other benefits, but EPA and DHA are also found directly in oily fish.

Superfoods

The term "superfoods" is used to describe foods that have particularly potent health benefits. They may contain a high level of vitamin C or be rich in heart-protecting soluble fiber, such as oats or lentils. However, the term is often used for a food that has high levels of plant compounds, which can have a strong antioxidant effect in our bodies. Experts have now found thousands of these compounds—with names such as flavonoids, polyphenols, carotenes, sulfides, and glucosinolates—that offer us protection from diseases, such as cancer, arthritis, and heart disease, and also help everyday well-being. Any diet that contains a wide variety of plant foods should be rich in "superfoods."

How can I be more healthy?

A balanced and varied diet is crucial to your well-being, but other lifestyle choices can have important roles to play, too. It is not only what you eat but also how much you eat that matters, as well as getting enough exercise into your daily routine. It is essential to know how to balance your energy intake—matching how many calories you eat or drink with how many you burn off during exercise. There are several tips you can use to help you achieve this energy balance without too much effort.

It is essential to know how to balance your energy intake—matching how many calories you eat or drink with how many you burn off.

Increase your exercise

Several worldwide studies have shown that many of us put on weight not because we are eating much more than we used to, but because we burn fewer calories through activity. We humans were designed to use our bodies—to walk, to run, to climb—but in the modern world it is easy to do very little. Cars, home appliances, the Internet, TV, office jobs, escalators, and elevators all help to keep us sedentary.

Exercise not only helps keep your weight stable (and can actually help you lose weight), it has many other benefits, too. It improves sleep patterns and insomnia, helps lift depression, keeps joints supple, improves posture, increases strength and mobility, improves heart and lung health, and can even decrease the risk of diabetes.

The best exercise is anything you enjoy doing and that you can do without huge expense or adjusting your life too much. Walking is ideal because it can be fitted in anywhere, is free, and every minute counts as exercise. Try taking the stairs not the elevator or walking one extra stop instead of taking the bus all the way. Also think about cycling, swimming, or even dancing in your living room. Do at least 30 minutes a day, five days a week.

Think about how you eat

In our busy lives, it is easy to grab a quick takeout or heat up a TV dinner. And if we're hungry between meals, it's hard to resist the temptation of buying a candy bar or a bag of potato chips.

However, if you want to eat a balanced and varied diet, you need to become more mindful of

these eating patterns and begin making little changes.

If you have been so busy that food has been taking a backseat in your life, think about small ways you can make it more important. For example, try to choose wisely and take more time over shopping, preparation, and eating your food. Food is, or should be, a pleasure, not a chore—so use it as a way to be kind to yourself.

Here are some other ideas you might use:

• Set aside 30 minutes or so at the weekend to plan some easy evening meal ideas you might like to try from this book, along with some healthy packed lunches you might take to work and some

quick, healthy breakfasts. Then, write your shopping list and enjoy a trip to the local stores to stock up. Home cooking can be a relaxing pleasure and it doesn't have to be difficult. The results will almost always be healthier and tastier than those takeouts.

• When you buy prepared foods, check the labels so that you choose items that will fit in with your exercise levels and calorie and nutrition needs (see page 9).

• Save money—watch your portion sizes when you cook. It's tempting to make a little extra "just in case," but only do that if you can make one and freeze one for another day. Research shows that cutting down portion sizes a little at most meals

is a great way to lose weight and keep it off.

• Eat regularly. It is better to eat small meals more frequently, for example, than to try to "be good" and have just one big meal. That often leads to binging and cravings, as well as making you feel dizzy or headachy. An ideal pattern is breakfast, lunch, a small late afternoon snack, and an evening meal. The eating plan on page 15 shows you how your day's menu might look.

• Take time to relax and enjoy your food—chew everything well and really enjoy it. Research shows you eat less if you do this instead of using a mealtime to work, read, or watch TV.

How do I use this book?

Now that you have a good understanding of what a healthy lifestyle is, you'll want to include many of our recipes in your diet in the weeks and months ahead. Check back to page 9. You will see the chart listing recommended amounts of the major nutrients. Now flick through our recipes and you'll see that each one contains nutritional information, so it is easy to keep track of whether you're eating too many calories each day, whether you're cutting down enough on, for example, salt, or if you're getting sufficient fiber in your diet.

There is also useful "flag" information in the top left of each recipe, telling you what particular types of diet each recipe can be used in and/or its special benefits. The flags are:

Super low calorie: This means the recipe is suitable for anyone on a weight-loss diet. If you pick a low-calorie flagged meal each day for breakfast, lunch, and dinner, as well as one flagged snack OR dessert, plus a one-cup milk allowance and unlimited salad greens and leafy greens, you will be eating no more than 1,350 calories—a suitable level to lose weight steadily until your target. Make sure, however, you don't eat too few calories—this would be less than 1,200 calories per day for a woman and less than 1,500 for a man.

Extra low sat fat: This means that the recipe contains less than 4g saturated fat per portion, which is well within the target set by health professionals for those people required to follow a low saturated fat diet.

Wheat, gluten, and dairy free: This flag means that the recipe contains no wheat, gluten, or dairy and, therefore, is suitable for people following a diet that excludes any or all of these items.

Fuller for longer: This flag is useful for people on a low-calorie diet, people who tend to get hungry, active people, or anyone who has diabetes or its precursor, prediabetes (or high blood glucose levels). These recipes are rich in the types of food that help regulate blood glucose. These foods are proteins, healthy fats, and certain high-fiber foods low on the glycemic index (an index showing the rate at which different foods are absorbed into the bloodstream). This flag shows that at least 50 percent of the calories in the recipe should come from nutrients that help you feel fuller for longer.

Low on carbs: These recipes contain low levels of starches and/or sugars (both types of carbohydrate). This flag is useful for people following a low-carbohydrate diet for health reasons or weight-loss purposes. This flag shows that less than 20 percent of the calories in this recipe come from carbohydrates.

Protein packed: Recipes flagged with this symbol are high protein and may be especially useful for people who prefer to diet or maintain their weight on a lower-carb, higher-protein plan. High-protein diets can help beat hunger and also speed the metabolic rate (the rate at which you burn calories). They are also useful if you are exercising to build lean muscles. This flag shows that at least 40 percent of the calories in the recipe are from protein.

Your week's food plan

This plan is suitable for an average woman for weight maintainance. It provides a balance of all the nutrients you need and is also within the guidelines for fat, saturated fat, sugars, and salt. So, for example, a meal that's higher in, say, fat (or salt or sugar) will be followed by one that's lower, and so a healthy balance is kept. We suggest that men should add extras, such as bread, potato, pasta, rice, noodles, nuts, seeds, and fruit, to add on the additional 600 or so calories they need each day.

You can also have a cup of skim, low-fat, or calcium-fortified soy milk every day, and don't forget to drink several glasses of water or herbal tea a day. Salad greens and leafy greens are unlimited, as are fresh herbs and spices and lemon juice. The recipes listed in the plan should be taken to be one serving of the recipe, unless stated otherwise.

Day One

Breakfast: Apricot & Apple Compote (page 30) with 1 tablespoon chopped nuts; ½ cup low-fat yogurt or soy yogurt; 1 thick slice whole-grain toast and 2 teaspoons unsalted low-fat spread.
Lunch: Chicken Noodle Bowl (page 82); 1 orange.
Snack: Grazing Mix (page 298); 1 large banana.
Dinner: Chunky Monkfish Casserole (page 160); ¾ cup mashed potatoed made with skim milk and low-fat spread; ½ cup steamed chopped broccoli; Coconut Rice Pudding (page 232).

Day Two

Breakfast: Banana Breakfast Shake (page 58); 8 almonds; 1 red-skinned apple.
Lunch: Red Pepper Hummus, Arugula & Artichoke Wraps (page 88).
Snack: 3 Beet Brownie Bites (page 306); ½ cup low-fat plain yogurt.
Dinner: Polenta Tart (page 190); 1 large bowl mixed leaf salad with 1 tablespoon French dressing; Fluffy Lemon Whips (page 228).

Day Three

Breakfast: Crunchy Brunch Wraps (page 60).
Lunch: "Shake It" Salad (page 76).
Snack: Grazing Mix (page 298); 1 large banana.
Dinner: Soy & Ginger Pork Tenderloin (page 140); 1¾ ounces whole-wheat noodles, cooked; Oaty Plum Crisp (page 264); 1 tablespoon low-fat plain yogurt.

Day Four

Breakfast: Breakfast Cookie (page 38); 1 large banana.
Lunch: Smoked Mackerel Salad (page 90); 1 thick slice whole-grain bread with 2 teaspoons unsalted low-fat spread; 1 orange.
Snack: Apple Dips (page 304).
Dinner: Tofu Steak with Fennel & Orange (page 180); Raw Beet & Pecan Side Salad (page 270); ⅓ cup bulgur wheat, cooked; Peach Popovers (page 224).

Day Five

Breakfast: Grape Pancake Stacks (page 36).
Lunch: Whole-Wheat Spaghetti with Edamame (page 92); 1 large bowl mixed leaf salad with 1 tablespoon French dressing.
Snack: Peanut Dip with Pita Chips (page 290).
Dinner: Chickpea & Spinach Salad (page 200); Vanilla Soufflé Omelet (page 222).

Day Six

Breakfast: Cherry & Almond Granola (page 28).
Lunch: Brown Rice with Asparagus (page 100); 1 orange.
Snack: Peanut Dip with Pita Chips (page 290) and vegetable sticks.
Dinner: Broiled Salmon with Mango & Lime Salsa (page 152); 8 ounces steamed new potatoes; ¾ cup steamed green beans; Golden Polenta Cake (page 236).

Day Seven

Breakfast: Spinach Scramble with Toasted Rye (page 50); 1 banana.
Lunch: Warm Shredded Beef Tabbouleh Salad (page 84).
Snack: Grazing Mix (page 298); 3 Beet Brownie Bites (page 306).
Dinner: Tempeh Noodle Bowl (page 194); Apple & Almond Roll (page 238).

Berry Sunrise Smoothie *18*

Strawberry Yogurt Dip *20*

Spicy Apple Oats *22*

Nectarine Crunch *24*

Apricot Oat Bars *26*

Cherry & Almond Granola *28*

Apricot & Apple Compote *30*

Cranberry & Seed Muesli *32*

Butternut Squash & Pecan Pancakes *34*

Grape Pancake Stacks *36*

Gluten- and Dairy-Free Breakfast Cookies *38*

Millet Porridge with Apricot Puree *40*

Zucchini Fritters *42*

Sausage & Potato Omelet *44*

Baked Mushrooms with Herb Ricotta *46*

Breakfast Burrito *48*

Spinach Scramble with Toasted Rye Bread *50*

Poached Eggs in Tomato Sauce *52*

Mushrooms on Toast *54*

Red Pepper Booster *56*

Banana Breakfast Shake *58*

Crunchy Brunch Wraps *60*

Whole-Wheat Muffins *62*

Raw Buckwheat & Almond Porridge *64*

Breakfasts & Brunches

Berry Sunrise Smoothie

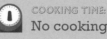

SERVES 1

PREP TIME:
5 minutes

COOKING TIME:
No cooking

nutritional information per serving	259 cal, 4g fat, 0.7g sat fat, 46g total sugars, trace salt, 4.5g fiber, 48g carbs, 9.5g protein

For a quick and filling pick-me-up before heading out of the door, this tasty smoothie can't be beaten.

INGREDIENTS

1 banana
¼ cup coarsely chopped, drained silken tofu,
¾ cup orange juice
1¾ cups frozen mixed berries

1. Coarsely chop the banana into smaller pieces.

2. Put all of the ingredients in a blender and process on high speed until smooth, or use a handheld immersion blender to process until smooth. Let the smoothie settle for a few seconds, then process again to completely blend.

3. Serve the smoothie immediately in a tall drinking glass.

1
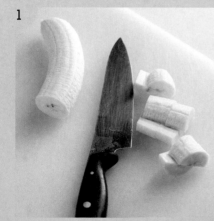

2

2

SOMETHING
DIFFERENT
Try using apple
juice instead of
orange juice for
a change—or
try apple cider
in the fall.

Fuller for longer

Extra low sat fat

Super low calorie

Strawberry Yogurt Dip

 SERVES 4

PREP TIME:
10 minutes

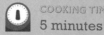 COOKING TIME:
5 minutes

nutritional information per serving	166 cal, 5g fat, 3g sat fat, 13g total sugars, 0.4g salt, 4g fiber, 24g carbs, 6.5g protein

This beautifully balanced dish is great for dieters and is rich in fiber, vitamin C, and antioxidants.

INGREDIENTS

⅔ cup coarsely chopped, hulled ripe strawberries, plus extra to garnish

1 tablespoon confectioners' sugar

1 cup fromage blanc or Greek yogurt

1 teaspoon lemon juice

4 slices whole-wheat bread

2 large pieces of fruit, such as a mango, nectarine, or banana, cut into wedges

1. Process the strawberries with the confectioners' sugar in a blender for a few seconds or mash with the sugar using a fork.

2. Combine the mixture with the fromage blanc or yogurt and lemon juice in a bowl. Spoon into a serving dish and chill, if you have time.

3. Toast the bread and cut into strips. Arrange the fruit as dippers on a plate around the strawberry dip. Garnish the dip with halves of fresh strawberries. Serve immediately, with the toast strips.

1   2   3

SOMETHING DIFFERENT
In the winter, you could replace the strawberries with ripe, chopped pears.

Fuller for longer

Extra low sat fat

Nectarine Crunch

🍴 SERVES 3   👨‍🍳 PREP TIME: 10–15 minutes   ⏲ COOKING TIME: No cooking

nutritional information per serving	400 cal, 11.5g fat, 2.5g sat fat, 44g total sugars, 0.2g salt, 6g fiber, 64g carbs, 15g protein

Serve this crunchy, fruity concoction as a speedily prepared brunch dish. Peaches make an excellent substitute for nectarines.

INGREDIENTS

4 nectarines

2 tablespoons peach preserves

2 tablespoons peach juice

1½ cups raisin and nut crunchy granola

1¼ cups low-fat plain yogurt

1. Cut the nectarines in half, then remove and discard the pits. Chop the flesh into bite-size pieces and reserve a few slices for decoration.

2. Put the preserves and peach juice in a bowl and mix together.

3. Place a few of the nectarine pieces in the bottom of three sundae glasses. Top with half of the granola and a spoonful of the yogurt. Add a few more of the nectarine pieces and spoon a little of the preserves mixture on top. Repeat the layers with the remaining ingredients, finishing with a spoonful of yogurt. Sprinkle any remaining granola over the top of each sundae.

4. Decorate with the reserved nectarine pieces and serve immediately.

1

2

3

Fuller for longer

Extra low sat fat

Super low calorie

Apricot Oat Bars

 MAKES 10

PREP TIME:
15 minutes

COOKING TIME:
20–25 minutes

nutritional information per bar	293 cal, 16.5g fat, 3g sat fat, 17g total sugars, 0.4g salt, 3g fiber, 32g carbs, 3.5g protein

Just one of these tasty oat bars gives you morning-long sustenance and is a great way to get iron and fiber.

INGREDIENTS

sunflower oil, for oiling
¾ cup low-fat spread
⅓ cup raw brown sugar
¼ cup honey
1 cup chopped dried apricots
2 teaspoons sesame seeds
2½ cups rolled oats

1. Preheat the oven to 350°F. Lightly oil an 11 x 7-inch shallow baking pan.

2. Put the spread, sugar, and honey into a small saucepan over low heat and heat until the ingredients have melted together—do not boil. When the ingredients are warm and well combined, stir in the apricots, sesame seeds, and oats.

3. Spoon the batter into the prepared pan and lightly level with the back of a spoon. Cook in the preheated oven for 20–25 minutes, or until golden brown. Remove from the oven, cut into 10 bars, and let cool completely before removing from the baking pan. Store the oat bars in an airtight container and consume within two to three days.

FREEZING TIP
After cutting the
oat bars, put into
a freezer bag
and store in the
freezer for up
to three months.

Fuller for longer

Extra low sat fat

Super low calorie

Cherry & Almond Granola

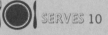

SERVES 10

PREP TIME:
15 minutes

COOKING TIME:
1¼–1½ hours

nutritional information per serving	242 cal, 11g fat, 3.5g sat fat, 14g total sugars, 0.1g salt, 5g fiber, 28g carbs, 6g protein

Plenty of crunch with just a touch of sweetness, this filling cereal will keep you going until lunchtime.

INGREDIENTS

1 spray vegetable oil spray
2½ cups rolled oats
¾ cup dried coconut
½ cup slivered almonds
½ cup ground flaxseed
¼ teaspoon salt
½ cup maple syrup
¼ cup water
1 tablespoon vegetable oil
1 teaspoon vanilla extract
⅔ cup chopped dried cherries

1. Preheat the oven to 275°F. Line a large baking sheet with parchment paper and spray it lightly with the vegetable oil spray.

2. In a large bowl, combine the oats, coconut, almonds, flaxseed, and salt and stir to mix well. In a small bowl, combine the maple syrup, water, vegetable oil, and vanilla extract. Pour the liquid mixture over the dry mixture and stir well. Pour the mixture onto the prepared baking sheet and spread out into an even layer.

3. Bake in the preheated oven for about 45 minutes, then stir well and spread out again into an even layer. Continue to bake for an additional 30–40 minutes, until crisp and beginning to color. Stir in the cherries and let cool to room temperature.

4. Store in a tightly covered container at room temperature for up to a week.

HEALTHY HINT
Replace the
coconut with the
same amount of
pumpkin seeds
for an even
healthier option.

Fuller for longer

Extra low sat fat

Super low calorie

Wheat, gluten
& dairy free

Apricot & Apple Compote

 SERVES 4

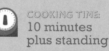 PREP TIME:
5 minutes

COOKING TIME:
10 minutes
plus standing

nutritional information per serving	163 cal, 0.4g fat, 0g sat fat, 39g total sugars, trace salt, 6g fiber, 41g carbs, 2g protein

Dried fruits are a concentrated package of vitamins, antioxidants, iron, and fiber—a perfect start to the day.

INGREDIENTS

¾ cup dried apricots
1 cup dried apple
⅓ cup raisins
1 vanilla bean, split lengthwise
1¼ cups apple juice
low-fat soy yogurt, to serve

1. Cut any large pieces of fruit in half. Put the apricots, apples, and raisins in a single layer in a skillet and add the vanilla bean.

2. Pour the apple juice over the dried fruit and put the skillet over medium heat. Heat gently until almost boiling. Remove from the heat, cover, and let stand for about 30 minutes, or until the fruit is plump and tender.

3. Remove the vanilla bean. Serve the compote immediately, with soy yogurt spooned over the top.

FREEZING TIP
This compote
freezes well for
three months. Put
in a freezerproof
container then seal
and freeze. Thaw
in the refrigerator
overnight.

Fuller for longer

Extra low sat fat

Cranberry & Seed Muesli

 SERVES 6

PREP TIME:
5 minutes
plus soaking

COOKING TIME:
No cooking

nutritional information per serving	330 cal, 13g fat, 2g sat fat, 14g total sugars, trace salt, 8g fiber, 36g carbs, 9g protein

If you are bored with dry, oversweetened muesli from a package, try this naturally sweetened alternative.

INGREDIENTS

2 cups rolled oats

⅓ cup rye flakes

⅓ cup whole, unblanched almonds, coarsely chopped

⅓ cup dried cranberries

2 tablespoons sunflower seeds

2 tablespoons pumpkin seeds

2 tablespoons flaxseed

2 Pippin or other crisp apples

1¾ cups apple juice, plus extra to pour

1. Put the oats, rye flakes, almonds, cranberries, sunflower seeds, pumpkin seeds, and flaxseed in a large bowl and stir well.

2. Core and coarsely grate the apples and stir thoroughly into the dry ingredients.

3. Stir in the apple juice, cover, and let soak for about an hour, or refrigerate overnight.

4. To serve, spoon the mixture into six serving bowls. Serve with a small pitcher of extra apple juice for pouring over the muesli.

1   2   3

BE PREPARED

Mix a large batch of the dry ingredients and store in an airtight container for up to four weeks, ready to add fresh apple and apple juice.

Butternut Squash & Pecan Pancakes

 SERVES 6

PREP TIME:
5 minutes

COOKING TIME:
30 minutes

nutritional information per serving	228 cal, 4.5g fat, 0.8g sat fat, 28g total sugars, 0.6g salt, 1.6g fiber, 43.7g carbs, 6g protein

Adding nuts and nutrient-rich butternut squash to these mouth-watering pancakes gives them a real health boost.

INGREDIENTS

1 cup plus 2 tablespoons all-purpose flour

2 tablespoons chopped pecans

¼ cup firmly packed light brown sugar

2 teaspoons baking powder

½ teaspoon cinnamon

¼ teaspoon salt

1 egg

1¼ cups low-fat buttermilk

¾ cup peeled, cooked, and mashed butternut squash or pumpkin puree

1 teaspoon vanilla extract

1 spray vegetable oil spray

½ cup maple syrup, to serve

1. In a medium bowl, combine the flour, pecans, brown sugar, baking powder, cinnamon, and salt. In a large bowl, whisk the egg, buttermilk, butternut squash, and vanilla extract. Whisk the dry ingredients into the wet ingredients and mix well.

2. Spray a nonstick skillet with the vegetable oil spray and heat over medium–high heat. When hot, ladle in the batter ¼ cup at a time to make 3–4-inch pancakes.

3. Cook for about 2–3 minutes, or until bubbles begin to burst in the top and the bottom is lightly colored. Flip over and cook for about an additional 2 minutes, or until the second side is lightly colored. Serve immediately with maple syrup.

1

1

3

HEALTHY HINT Use whole-wheat flour to increase the fiber content.

Extra low sat fat

Super low calorie

Grape Pancake Stacks

 SERVES 4

PREP TIME:
10 minutes

COOKING TIME:
20 minutes

nutritional information per serving	235 cal, 5g fat, 1g sat fat, 14g total sugars, 0.5g salt, 2g fiber, 44g carbs, 6g protein

These dairy-free fruit pancakes are easy to make and take just minutes to cook.

INGREDIENTS

1¼ cups all-purpose flour

1½ teaspoons baking powder

1 cup white grape juice

1 extra-large egg

1 cup halved or quartered red seedless grapes

sunflower oil, for brushing

sprigs of grapes, to serve

1. Sift together the flour and baking powder into a large bowl. Add the grape juice and egg, then whisk to a smooth, bubbly batter. Stir in the grapes.

2. Preheat a flat griddle pan or large, heavy skillet over high heat until hot and brush lightly with oil. Reduce the heat to medium and, using a small ladle, pour three separate scoops of the batter onto the hot pan.

3. Cook for 1–2 minutes, or until just set and golden underneath. Flip over with a spatula and cook the other side for about 1 minute, or until golden underneath. Set aside and keep warm. Repeat with the remaining batter until you have about 20 pancakes.

4. Stack the pancakes on warm plates. Serve each stack with a few grapes and serve immediately.

1   2   3

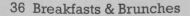

BE PREPARED
The batter can be prepared several hours in advance. Prepare to the end of step 1, cover, and store in the refrigerator until ready to cook.

Fuller for longer

Wheat, gluten & dairy free

Gluten- and Dairy-Free Breakfast Cookies

 MAKES 6

PREP TIME:
10–15 minutes

COOKING TIME:
12–15 minutes

nutritional information per cookie	318 cal, 17g fat, 5.5g sat fat, 24g total sugars, 0.2g salt, 2.5g fiber, 40g carbs, 5.5g protein

These wheat, dairy, and gluten-free cookies are great for a sustaining breakfast on the run.

INGREDIENTS

sunflower oil, for greasing

1 cup Brazil nuts

⅔ cup confectioners' sugar

¾ cup buckwheat flour

½ teaspoon gluten-free baking powder

½ teaspoon xanthan gum

½ cup golden raisins

⅓ cup dried coconut

2 egg whites

poppy seeds and dark brown sugar, to sprinkle

1. Preheat the oven to 350°F. Lightly grease a large baking sheet.

2. Put the Brazil nuts, confectioners' sugar, and buckwheat flour in a food processor and process until finely ground. Transfer the mixture to a large bowl, then stir in the baking powder and xanthan gum.

3. Stir in the golden raisins, coconut, and egg whites and combine thoroughly, using your hands, until a soft, sticky dough forms.

4. Divide the dough into six and roll each piece into a ball. Place on the prepared baking sheet and press each ball with your fingers to create 4½-inch circles. Sprinkle lightly with poppy seeds and brown sugar.

5. Bake in the preheated oven for 12–15 minutes, or until firm and just beginning to brown. Let cool on the baking sheet before serving.

2

4

4

SOMETHING
DIFFERENT
For a change of
flavor, replace the golden
raisins with an equal
amount of chopped
dried apricots and the
Brazils with chopped
blanched almonds.

Millet Porridge with Apricot Puree

 SERVES 4

PREP TIME:
5 minutes

COOKING TIME:
25 minutes

nutritional information per serving	289 cal, 3g fat, 1g sat fat, 12g total sugars, 0.6g salt, 2.5g fiber, 52g carbs, 4.5g protein

Gluten-free millet makes a good replacement for oats and the apricots will boost your iron intake for the day.

INGREDIENTS

5½ cups millet flakes
2 cups soy milk
pinch of salt
freshly grated nutmeg, to serve

apricot puree
1 cup coarsely chopped dried apricots
1¼ cups water

1. To make the apricot puree, put the apricots into a saucepan and cover with the water. Bring to a boil, then reduce the heat and simmer, half covered, for 20 minutes, until the apricots are tender. Use a handheld immersion blender or transfer the apricots, along with any water left in the saucepan, to a food processor or blender and process until smooth. Set aside.

2. To make the porridge, put the millet flakes into a saucepan and add the milk and salt. Bring to a boil, then reduce the heat and simmer for 5 minutes, stirring frequently, until cooked and creamy.

3. To serve, spoon into four bowls and top with the apricot puree and a little nutmeg.

COOK'S NOTE *Boiling the apricots makes them plump for a smooth purée.*

Fuller for longer

Extra low sat fat

Super low calorie

Zucchini Fritters

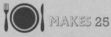 MAKES 25

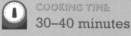 PREP TIME: 10 minutes

COOKING TIME: 30–40 minutes

nutritional information per fritter	28 cal, 1g fat, 0.3g sat fat, 0.3g total sugars, trace salt, 0.3g fiber, 3g carbs, 1g protein

Quick to make, these fritters are ideal for a filling start to the day. To save time, you could prepare the batter the night before. Beat well before adding the zucchini, adding a little more milk, if needed.

INGREDIENTS

¾ cup all-purpose flour
¾ teaspoon baking powder
2 eggs, beaten
¼ cup milk
1½ zucchini
2 tablespoons fresh thyme
1 tablespoon sunflower oil
salt and pepper, to taste

1. Sift the flour and baking powder into a large bowl and make a well in the center. Add the eggs to the well and, using a wooden spoon, gradually draw in the flour.

2. Slowly add the milk to the mixture, stirring continuously to form a thick batter.

3. Meanwhile, shred the zucchini over paper towels placed in a bowl to absorb some of the juices.

4. Add the zucchini, thyme, and salt and pepper to the batter and mix thoroughly, for about a minute.

5. Heat the oil in a large, heavy skillet. Taking a tablespoon of the batter for a medium-size fritter, spoon the batter into the hot oil and cook, in batches, for 3–4 minutes on each side.

6. Remove the fritters with a slotted spoon and drain thoroughly on absorbent paper towels. Keep each batch warm in the oven while making the rest. Allow five fritters per person and serve immediately.

Fuller for longer

Extra low sat fat

Wheat, gluten
& dairy free

Sausage & Potato Omelet

 SERVES 4

 PREP TIME:
10 minutes

COOKING TIME:
20–25 minutes

nutritional information per serving	330 cal, 12.5g fat, 2.5g sat fat, 7.5g total sugars, 1g salt, 6.5g fiber, 38g carbs, 16g protein

All the flavor and color of a cooked breakfast in one easy, healthy, low-fat, high-protein omelet—yum!

INGREDIENTS

4 wheat, gluten, and dairy-free sausages (meat or vegetarian)

sunflower oil, for frying

4 boiled potatoes, cooled and diced

8 cherry tomatoes

4 eggs, beaten

salt and pepper, to taste

1. Preheat the broiler to medium–high. Arrange the sausages on an aluminum foil-lined broiler pan and cook under the preheated broiler, turning occasionally, for 12–15 minutes, or until cooked through and golden brown. Let cool slightly, then slice into bite-size pieces.

2. Meanwhile, heat a little oil in a large, heavy skillet with a heatproof handle over medium heat. Add the potatoes and cook until golden brown and crisp all over, then add the tomatoes and cook for an additional 2 minutes. Arrange the sausages in the skillet so that there is an even distribution of potatoes, tomatoes, and sausages.

3. Add a little more oil to the skillet if it seems dry. Season the beaten eggs with salt and pepper and pour the mixture over the ingredients in the skillet. Cook for 3 minutes, without stirring or disturbing the eggs. Place the skillet under the preheated broiler for 3 minutes, or until the top is just cooked. Cut into wedges to serve.

1

2

3

SOMETHING
DIFFERENT
Try replacing
the sausage
with chopped
mushrooms or
shredded spinach.

Low on carbs

Fuller for longer

Extra low sat fat

Super low calorie

Baked Mushrooms with Herb Ricotta

 SERVES 4

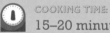 PREP TIME: 10 minutes

COOKING TIME: 15–20 minutes

nutritional information per serving	86 cal, 7g fat, 3g sat fat, 1g total sugars, 0.1g salt, 1.5g fiber, 1g carbs, 5g protein

Ricotta cheese is relatively low in fat in comparison with other cheeses and is a good source of protein and calcium.

INGREDIENTS

4 large, flat mushrooms
1 tablespoon olive oil
1 shallot, coarsely chopped
1 cup fresh flat-leaf parsley
1 tablespoon snipped fresh chives
1 cup ricotta cheese
salt and pepper, to taste

1. Preheat the oven to 400°F. Remove the stems from the mushrooms and set aside. Put the mushrooms in a shallow baking dish and brush with the oil.

2. Put the mushroom stems, shallot, parsley, and chives in a food processor and blend until finely chopped. Season with salt and pepper.

3. Put the chopped ingredients in a large bowl with the ricotta and stir to mix evenly.

4. Spoon the herb ricotta onto the top of the mushrooms. Bake in the preheated oven for 15–20 minutes, or until tender and bubbling. Serve immediately.

GOES WELL WITH
Chunky slices of
sourdough bread,
either plain or
toasted, make
a really good
accompaniment to
the mushrooms
and soak up the
tasty juices.

Fuller for longer

Extra low sat fat

Super low calorie

Breakfast Burrito

 SERVES 1

 PREP TIME: 5 minutes

 COOKING TIME: 5 minutes

nutritional information per serving	288 cal, 6g fat, 2.5g sat fat, 4g total sugars, 2.8g salt, 6g fiber, 47g carbs, 15g protein

This breakfast has fiber, protein, and carbohydrates to keep you feeling full, and a hit of vitamin C, too.

INGREDIENTS

2 egg whites

pinch of salt

¼ teaspoon pepper

1 scallion, thinly sliced

1 spray vegetable oil spray

¼ cup diced red or green bell pepper

2 tablespoons drained and rinsed, canned black beans

1 whole-wheat flour tortilla, warm

2 tablespoons crumbled feta cheese

2 tablespoons salsa

1 teaspoon finely chopped fresh cilantro, plus extra leaves to garnish

1. In a small bowl, combine the egg whites, salt, pepper, and scallion and stir well.

2. Spray a nonstick skillet with vegetable oil spray and put it over medium–high heat. Add the red bell pepper and cook, stirring, for about 3 minutes, or until it begins to soften. Reduce the heat to medium, pour in the egg mixture, and cook, stirring often, for an additional 1–2 minutes, or until the egg sets.

3. Put the beans in a microwave-safe bowl and microwave on high for about 1 minute, or until heated through.

4. Spoon the cooked egg mixture onto the tortilla. Top with the beans, cheese, salsa, and cilantro. Serve immediately, garnished with whole cilantro leaves.

Low on carbs

Fuller for longer

Spinach Scramble with Toasted Rye Bread

 SERVES 4

PREP TIME: 5 minutes

COOKING TIME: 5–6 minutes

nutritional information per serving	300 cal, 19g fat, 6g sat fat, 1.5g total sugars, 1.1g salt, 3g fiber, 13g carbs, 21g protein

Rye bread has a rich, nutty flavor and is higher in nutrients than bread made with wheat flour.

INGREDIENTS

1 (6-ounce) package young spinach leaves, coarsely shredded

8 extra-large eggs

3 tablespoons skim milk

1 tablespoon butter

4 slices rye bread

salt and pepper, to taste

freshly grated nutmeg, to serve

1. Heat a large skillet or wok over high heat and add the spinach. Stir for 1–2 minutes, or until the leaves are wilted. Remove from the heat, transfer to a strainer, and squeeze out as much of the excess moisture as possible. Set aside and keep warm.

2. Break the eggs into a bowl, add the milk, and season with salt and pepper. Beat lightly with a fork until evenly mixed.

3. Melt the butter in the skillet or wok over medium heat. Add the eggs and stir until just beginning to set. Add the spinach and stir until lightly set.

4. Meanwhile, lightly toast the rye bread.

5. Spoon the spinach scramble over the toast, sprinkle with nutmeg, and serve immediately.

1

2

3

HEALTHY HINT
If you're on a low-fat diet, replace the butter with your favorite low-fat spread.

Fuller for longer

Super low calorie

Poached Eggs in Tomato Sauce

 SERVES 4

PREP TIME:
10 minutes

COOKING TIME:
30–35 minutes

nutritional information per serving	299 cal, 16g fat, 5g sat fat, 4.5g total sugars, 1.6g salt, 4g fiber, 21g carbs, 17g protein

This rustic egg dish is perfect for brunch, but it's satisfying enough to hold its own at lunch as well.

INGREDIENTS

1 tablespoon olive oil

1 small onion, diced

2 garlic cloves, finely chopped

½ teaspoon salt

½ teaspoon pepper

¼ teaspoon crushed red pepper flakes

¼ cup red wine

1 (14½-ounce) can diced tomatoes, with juice

2 teaspoons finely chopped fresh oregano, thyme, basil, sage, or other fresh herb

4 eggs

4 slices toasted whole-wheat country-style bread, to serve

2 tablespoons finely chopped Kalamata olives, to serve

½ cup grated Parmesan cheese, to serve

1. Heat the oil in a large skillet over medium–high heat. Add the onion and garlic and cook, stirring occasionally, for about 5 minutes, or until soft. Add the salt, pepper, red pepper flakes, and wine and cook for an additional few minutes, until the liquid has mostly evaporated. Add the tomatoes and their juice, bring to a boil, then reduce the heat to medium–low and simmer for about 15–20 minutes, or until the sauce thickens. Stir in the fresh herbs.

2. Make four wells in the sauce and carefully crack the eggs into them. Cover and simmer for about 7–9 minutes, or until the whites are set but the yolks are still runny.

3. Put the toast slices on four serving plates. Carefully scoop the eggs out of the sauce and place one on each slice of toast. Place spoonfuls of the sauce around the egg and top with a sprinkling of chopped olives and Parmesan cheese. Serve immediately.

Mushrooms on Toast

 SERVES 4   PREP TIME: 10 minutes   COOKING TIME: 10 minutes

nutritional information per serving	352 cal, 11g fat, 1.5g sat fat, 3g total sugars, 1.6g salt, 5g fiber, 53g carbs, 11g protein

Wild and dark mushrooms provide the antioxidant mineral selenium, as well as other immune-boosting chemicals.

INGREDIENTS

4 large slices French-style bread, each ½ inch thick, or 2 individual baguettes, cut lengthwise

3 tablespoons olive oil

2 garlic cloves, crushed

3 cups sliced cremini mushrooms

8 ounces mixed wild mushrooms

2 teaspoons lemon juice

2 tablespoons chopped fresh flat-leaf parsley

salt and pepper, to taste

1. Put the slices of bread on a ridged grill pan and toast on both sides until golden. Reserve and keep warm.

2. Meanwhile, heat the oil in a skillet. Add the garlic and cook gently for a few seconds, then add the cremini mushrooms. Cook, stirring continuously, over high heat for 3 minutes. Add the wild mushrooms and cook for an additional 2 minutes. Stir in the lemon juice.

3. Season with salt and pepper and stir in the chopped parsley.

4. Spoon the mushroom mixture over the top of the warm toast and serve immediately.

1   2   3

SOMETHING
DIFFERENT
Look for packages
of mixed mushrooms,
which are ideal for
this recipe.

Red Pepper Booster

🍽 SERVES 2   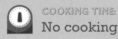 PREP TIME: 5 minutes   COOKING TIME: No cooking

nutritional information per serving	113 cal, 0.9g fat, 0g sat fat, 22g total sugars, 0.9g salt, 5g fiber, 22g carbs, 4g protein

Pour yourself a glass of goodness! This is the perfect choice for a healthier drink option and will look really inviting served in a pitcher with ice cubes.

INGREDIENTS

1 cup carrot juice

1 cup tomato juice

2 large red bell peppers, seeded and coarsely chopped

1 tablespoon lemon juice

pepper, to taste

lemon slices, to garnish

1. Pour the carrot juice and tomato juice into a food processor or blender and process gently until combined.

2. Add the red bell peppers and lemon juice. Season with plenty of pepper and process until smooth. Pour the mixture into glasses, garnish with lemon slices, and serve.

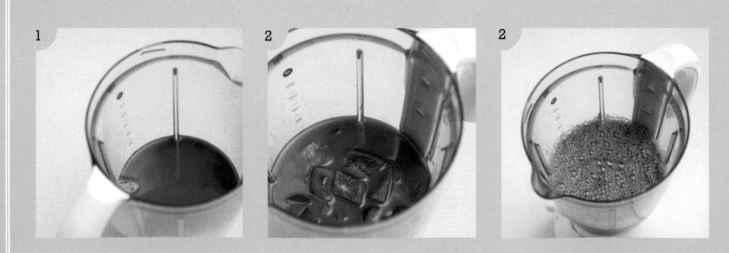

SOMETHING
DIFFERENT
Have some hot
pepper sauce
available to
add some heat,
if desired.

Fuller for longer

Crunchy Brunch Wraps

 SERVES 4   PREP TIME: 10 minutes   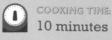 COOKING TIME: 10 minutes

nutritional information per serving	390 cal, 21g fat, 6g sat fat, 2g total sugars, 2.3g salt, 3g fiber, 32.5g carbs, 20.5g protein

These healthy but hearty brunch wraps are easy to eat on the go and contain enough nutrition to keep you going until the afternoon.

INGREDIENTS

4 eggs
5 ounces lean pancetta cubes
4 soft corn tortillas
3 cups baby spinach leaves
2 tablespoons pumpkin seeds, toasted

dressing

2 tablespoons fresh orange juice
2 tablespoons low-fat plain yogurt
salt and pepper, to taste

1. Place the eggs in a saucepan of cold water, then put over high heat and bring to a boil. Reduce the heat and simmer gently for 8 minutes. Drain the eggs, crack the shells, and put under cold running water for 2 minutes. Peel off the shells and cut the eggs into quarters.

2. Meanwhile, put a heavy skillet over medium–high heat. Sauté the pancetta cubes, stirring occasionally, for about 5 minutes, or until golden brown and the fat runs out. Remove the cubes with a slotted spoon and drain well on absorbent paper towels.

3. Put the four corn tortillas on a work surface and divide the spinach leaves among them. Top with the egg quarters and sprinkle with the pancetta and pumpkin seeds.

4. To make the dressing, stir together the orange juice and yogurt in a small bowl and season with salt and pepper. Drizzle the dressing over the ingredients in the tortilla and fold up the wraps. Serve immediately.

Fuller for longer

Extra low sat fat

Super low calorie

Wheat, gluten
& dairy free

Raw Buckwheat & Almond Porridge

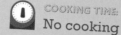 SERVES 6

PREP TIME:
15 minutes plus
soaking & chilling

COOKING TIME:
No cooking

nutritional information per serving	288 cal, 8g fat, 1g sat fat, 0.7g total sugars, trace salt, 6g fiber, 45g carbs, 5.5g protein

Packed with magnesium for your heart, this is also rich in delicious nutty buckwheat, an ideal grain substitute.

INGREDIENTS

almond milk
½ cup whole raw almonds, soaked overnight in water

1¼ cups water

porridge
2 cups raw buckwheat groats, soaked in cold water for 90 minutes

1 teaspoon cinnamon

2 tablespoons light agave nectar or syrup, plus extra to serve

sliced strawberries, to serve

1. To make the almond milk, drain the almonds and transfer to a blender or food processor. Blend the almonds with the water. Keep the blender running for a minute or two to break down the almonds as much as possible.

2. Pour the mixture into a strainer lined with cheesecloth and squeeze through as much of the liquid as possible into a large bowl. You should get about 1¼ cups of raw almond milk.

3. Rinse the soaked buckwheat thoroughly in cold water. Transfer to the blender or food processor with the almond milk, cinnamon, and agave nectar. Blend to a slightly coarse texture.

4. Chill the mixture for at least 30 minutes or overnight. It can be stored, covered, in the refrigerator for 3 days.

5. Serve in small bowls, topped with sliced strawberries and agave nectar to taste.

Light Lunches

Minestrone Soup

Fuller for longer

Extra low sat fat

Super low calorie

 SERVES 4

 PREP TIME:
15 minutes

COOKING TIME:
30–35 minutes

nutritional information per serving	99 cal, 1g fat, 0.2g sat fat, 9g total sugars, 1.2g salt, 5g fiber, 19g carbs, 6g protein

This delicious Italian soup is bursting with carotenes, which fight cancer and heart disease.

INGREDIENTS

2 sprays olive oil

1 onion, finely chopped

1 cup diced carrot

2 celery stalks, sliced

1 bouquet garni
(sprigs of parsley, thyme,
and a bay leaf tied together)

1 (14½-ounce) can diced tomatoes

2 ounces dried soup pasta
or spaghetti broken into
short lengths

3½ cups vegetable stock

½ head of small cabbage

pepper, to taste

1. Heat the oil in a large saucepan, add the onion, carrot, and celery, and sauté gently for 5 minutes, stirring frequently. Add the bouquet garni with the diced tomatoes. Fill the empty tomato can halfway with water, swirl to remove all the remaining tomatoes, then pour into the pan.

2. Add the pasta with the stock and bring to a boil. Reduce the heat to a simmer and cook for 12 minutes, or until the vegetables are almost tender.

3. Discard any outer leaves and hard central core from the cabbage and shred. Wash well, then add to the saucepan and season with pepper. Continue to cook for 5–8 minutes, or until all the vegetables are tender but still firm to the bite. Discard the bouquet garni and serve divided equally between four warm bowls.

HEALTHY HINT

Increase the protein content by adding a can of drained cooked navy beans with the cabbage.

Low on carbs

Protein packed

Fuller for longer

Extra low sat fat

Super low calorie

Mediterranean Fish Soup

 SERVES 4

 PREP TIME:
10 minutes

COOKING TIME:
20 minutes

nutritional information per serving	233 cal, 5g fat, 0.8g sat fat, 5g total sugars, 1.2g salt, 1.5g fiber, 6g carbs, 40g protein

Packed with protein to keep hunger pangs away, this is also rich in immune-boosting zinc and plant compounds.

INGREDIENTS

1 tablespoon olive oil

1 large onion, chopped

2 garlic cloves, finely chopped

2 cups fish stock

⅔ cup dry white wine

1 bay leaf

1 sprig each fresh thyme, rosemary and oregano

1 pound firm white fish fillets (such as red snapper, cod, monkfish, or halibut), skinned and cut into 1-inch cubes

1 pound fresh mussels, prepared

1 (14½-ounce) can diced tomatoes

8 ounces cooked, peeled shrimp

salt and pepper, to taste

fresh thyme sprigs, to garnish

French bread, to serve

1. Heat the olive oil in a large saucepan and gently sauté the onion and garlic for 2–3 minutes, or until just softened.

2. Pour in the stock and wine and bring to a boil. Tie the bay leaf and herbs together with clean string and add to the saucepan together with the fish and mussels. Stir well, cover, and simmer for 5 minutes.

3. Stir in the tomatoes and shrimp and continue to cook for another 3–4 minutes, or until piping hot and the fish is cooked through.

4. Discard the herbs and any mussels that have not opened. Season with salt and pepper, then ladle into warm bowls. Garnish with sprigs of fresh thyme and serve with French bread.

Carrot & Cumin Soup

Extra low sat fat

Super low calorie

 SERVES 2

PREP TIME:
15 minutes

 COOKING TIME:
35–40 minutes

nutritional information per serving	135 cal, 1g fat, 0.1g sat fat, 15g total sugars, 0.1g salt, 7g fiber, 15g carbs, 3g protein

A high-fiber soup that is ideal for dieters, this is also rich in vitamin A, essential for healthy skin.

INGREDIENTS

1 carrot, finely chopped

1 garlic clove, chopped

1 shallot, finely chopped

1 ripe tomato, skinned and chopped

½ teaspoon ground cumin

1 cup vegetable stock

1 bouquet garni (sprigs of parsley, thyme, and a bay leaf tied together)

2 teaspoons dry sherry (optional)

pepper, to taste

pinch of cumin and 1 tablespoon reduced-fat crème fraîche or Greek yogurt (optional), to garnish

1. Put the carrot, garlic, shallot, tomato, cumin, stock, and bouquet garni in a lidded saucepan.

2. Bring to a simmering point over high heat, then reduce the heat and simmer for 30 minutes, or until the vegetables are tender. Let cool slightly and remove the bouquet garni.

3. Pour the soup into a food processor or blender and puree until smooth.

4. Return to the saucepan, add the sherry, if using, and reheat gently. Season with pepper. Remove from the heat and ladle into warm mugs or bowls. Garnish with cumin and a swirl of crème fraîche or Greek yogurt, if using, and serve.

1   2   3

GOES WELL WITH
A slice of whole-grain bread will provide additional calories and the B vitamins.

Roasted Tomato Soup

Fuller for longer

Extra low sat fat

Super low calorie

 SERVES 4

PREP TIME:
25 minutes

COOKING TIME:
1¼ hours

nutritional information per serving	263 cals, 15g fat, 3.5g sat fat, 12g total sugars, 2g salt, 7g fiber, 26g carbs, 9g protein

This tangy soup is a source of sulfides from the onion and garlic, both of which are natural antibiotics.

INGREDIENTS

3 pounds plum tomatoes, halved (about 8 cups)

1 red onion, coarsely chopped

6 garlic cloves, peeled

2 tablespoons olive oil

¾ teaspoon salt

1 teaspoon pepper

6 sprigs fresh thyme, plus extra to garnish

4 cups vegetable stock

2 tablespoons lemon juice

parmesan croutons

3½ slices whole-wheat bread, cubed

2 tablespoons olive oil

½ teaspoon salt

¼ teaspoon pepper

2 tablespoons Parmesan cheese

1. Preheat the oven to 450°F. Toss the tomatoes, onion, and garlic on a large baking sheet with the olive oil, salt, pepper, and thyme. Spread the vegetables out into a single layer, arranging the tomatoes cut side up, and roast in the preheated oven for about 45 minutes, or until the vegetables are soft.

2. To make the croutons, reduce the oven heat to 300°F. Toss the cubed bread with the olive oil and sprinkle with the salt and pepper. Spread the bread cubes in an even layer on a baking sheet and bake in the preheated oven for about 25 minutes. Sprinkle with the cheese, return to the oven, and bake for an additional 5 minutes, or until the cheese is melted and beginning to brown.

3. Finish the soup while the croutons are baking. Puree the vegetables along with the stock, in several batches, in a blender or food processor. Alternatively, puree the vegetables and stock in a large saucepan using a handheld immersion blender.

4. Bring the soup to a boil in a large saucepan over high heat. Reduce the heat to medium and simmer, stirring occasionally, for about 15 minutes. Just before serving, stir in the lemon juice. Serve in warm bowls, garnished with croutons and thyme sprigs.

"Shake It" Salad

Fuller for longer

Extra low sat fat

Super low calorie

Wheat, gluten & dairy free

 SERVES 4

PREP TIME: 10 minutes

COOKING TIME: No cooking

nutritional information per serving	144 cal, 9g fat, 1g sat fat, 13g total sugars, trace salt, 4g fiber, 15g carbs, 2g protein

Seed and bean sprouts boost the nutritional content of this salad, which is ideal for taking to work or school.

INGREDIENTS

2 Pippin or other crisp red apples
lime juice, for sprinkling
1 large carrot
2½-inch piece cucumber
¾ cup bean sprouts
½ cup sunflower sprouts
1 cup alfalfa sprouts

dressing
1 tablespoon lime juice
3 tablespoons olive oil
1 teaspoon grated fresh ginger
1 teaspoon light brown sugar
salt and pepper, to taste

1. Core, quarter, and coarsely grate the apples into a bowl, then sprinkle with lime juice to prevent them from browning. Coarsely grate the carrot and the cucumber into two separate bowls.

2. To make the dressing, put all of the dressing ingredients in a jar or sealable food container, large enough to hold the salad with room to spare. Shake well to mix. Alternatively, make individual salads in four small jars.

3. Add all the bean and seed sprouts to the jar, then layer the apple, carrot and cucumber into the jar. Replace the lid until required.

4. To serve, shake the jar to coat the ingredients in the dressing, then either eat straight from the jar or transfer to bowls to serve.

1. 2. 3.

COOK'S NOTE

To sprout the seeds, soak overnight in a jar of cold water, drain, then rinse and drain twice a day for three to five days until sprouted.

Fuller for longer

Extra low sat fat

Super low calorie

Mixed Green Salad with Yogurt Dressing

SERVES 4

PREP TIME: 15 minutes

COOKING TIME: No cooking

nutritional information per serving	109 cal, 7g fat, 1.5g sat fat, 8.5g total sugars, 0.2g salt, 2.5g fiber, 8.5g carbs, 3g protein

Just what the doctor ordered to boost your vitamin C intake, this salad is zinging with fresh flavors.

INGREDIENTS

¾ cup sliced cucumber

6 scallions, chopped

2 tomatoes, sliced

1 yellow bell pepper, seeded and cut into strips

2 celery stalks, cut into strips

4 radishes, sliced

3 cups arugula

1 tablespoon chopped fresh mint, to garnish (optional)

dressing

2 tablespoons lemon juice

1 garlic clove, crushed

⅔ cup low-fat plain yogurt

2 tablespoons olive oil

salt and pepper, to taste

1. To make the salad, gently mix the cucumber, scallions, tomatoes, yellow bell pepper strips, celery, radishes, and arugula in a large serving bowl.

2. To make the dressing, stir together the lemon juice, garlic, plain yogurt, and olive oil in a small bowl until thoroughly combined. Season with salt and pepper.

3. Spoon the dressing over the salad and toss to mix. Garnish the salad with chopped mint, if using, and serve.

Fuller for longer

Super low calorie

Lentil & Goat Cheese Tomatoes

SERVES 4

PREP TIME:
15 minutes

COOKING TIME:
35–45 minutes

nutritional information per serving	182 cal, 10g fat, 5g sat fat, 7g total sugars, 0.5g salt, 4.5g fiber, 13.5g carbs, 10g protein

Lentils are a good source of protein and soluble fiber, which helps lower blood cholesterol.

INGREDIENTS

¼ cup dried green lentils

4 beefsteak tomatoes

1 tablespoon olive oil

2 large shallots, finely chopped

1 garlic clove, crushed

1 tablespoon chopped fresh thyme

4 ounces hard goat cheese, diced

salt and pepper, to taste

mixed salad, to serve

1. Bring a small saucepan of water to a boil over medium–high heat. Add the lentils, return to a boil, and cook for 20–25 minutes, or according to the package directions, until tender. Drain well.

2. Meanwhile, preheat the oven to 400°F. Cut a slice from the tops of the tomatoes and set aside. Scoop out the pulp from the center and coarsely chop.

3. Heat the oil in a skillet over medium heat and sauté the shallots, stirring, for 3–4 minutes to soften. Add the garlic and chopped tomato pulp and cook for an additional 3–4 minutes, or until any excess moisture has evaporated.

4. Place the tomatoes in a shallow baking dish. Stir the lentils and thyme into the skillet, and season with salt and pepper. Stir in the goat cheese and then spoon the mixture into the tomatoes.

5. Replace the lids on the tomatoes and bake in the preheated oven for 15–20 minutes, or until tender. Serve immediately, with mixed salad.

2

3

4

GOES WELL WITH

A crisp green
salad of
shredded lettuce
and sliced
cucumber makes
a refreshing
accompaniment to
the tomatoes.

Protein packed

Fuller for longer

Extra low sat fat

Chicken Noodle Bowl

 SERVES 4

 PREP TIME:
10 minutes

COOKING TIME:
10–15 minutes

nutritional information per serving	382 cal, 7g fat, 2g sat fat, 4g total sugars, 1.4g salt, 4g fiber, 41g carbs, 44g protein

This quick and easy, low-fat lunch dish is a great standby when time is tight.

INGREDIENTS

2½ cups low-sodium chicken stock

1 small green chile, seeded and chopped

1 garlic clove, finely chopped

2 pounds boneless, skinless chicken breasts, cut into strips

1 teaspoon Thai fish sauce

1 bunch scallions, chopped

8 ounces dried medium egg noodles

2 cups fresh bean sprouts

salt and pepper, to taste

1. Put the chicken stock into a large saucepan over medium–high heat and add the chile and garlic. Bring to a boil.

2. Stir in the strips of chicken and bring back to a boil, then reduce the heat slightly and simmer for 5 minutes. Add the fish sauce and scallions.

3. Add the egg noodles and simmer for about 4 minutes, stirring occasionally, or until the noodles are just tender.

4. Stir in the bean sprouts and heat for about a minute, then season with salt and pepper. Serve immediately in bowls.

2   3   4

COOK'S NOTE
If you are using bouillon cubes, be careful when adjusting the seasoning with salt because bouillon cubes can be salty.

Fuller for longer

Extra low sat fat

Super low calorie

Warm Shredded Beef Tabbouleh Salad

 SERVES 4

 PREP TIME:
10 minutes
plus standing

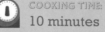 COOKING TIME:
10 minutes

nutritional information per serving	329 cal, 13g fat, 3.5g sat fat, 4g total sugars, 0.2g salt, 4.5g fiber, 26g carbs, 27g protein

A special salad for a summer lunch party or simply for a tasty treat when you need one.

INGREDIENTS

¾ cup bulgur wheat

1 pound lean tenderloin steak

3⅓ cups finely chopped fresh flat-leaf parsley

3 cups finely chopped fresh mint

1 red onion, thinly sliced

2 tomatoes, diced

1 tablespoon extra virgin olive oil, plus extra for brushing

juice of 2 lemons

salt and pepper, to taste

1. Put the bulgur wheat in a bowl and pour boiling water over the grains to cover. Let soak for 10 minutes. Drain thoroughly, pressing out any excess moisture.

2. Meanwhile, put a ridged grill pan or skillet over high heat. Season the steak with salt and pepper, brush lightly with oil, and cook for 2–3 minutes on each side, turning once. Remove from the heat and cover with aluminum foil for 5 minutes.

3. Mix together the parsley, mint, onion, tomatoes, and bulgur wheat in a bowl. Stir in the olive oil and lemon juice and season with salt and pepper.

4. Slice the steak into 1-inch thin strips. Transfer the bulgur wheat salad to warm plates, arrange the steak slices on top, then pour over the meat juices and serve.

HEALTHY HINT

If you are trying to reduce fat in your diet, you can omit the oil, although the flavor will not be as rich.

Fuller for longer

Extra low sat fat

Red Pepper Hummus, Arugula & Artichoke Wraps

 SERVES 4

PREP TIME:
10 minutes
plus cooling

COOKING TIME:
5–10 minutes

nutritional information per serving	350 cal, 13g fat, 1.5g sat fat, 5g total sugars, 1.6g salt, 11g fiber, 50g carbs, 12g protein

A variation on classic hummus using roasted bell peppers, which add a rich, sweet flavor, and extra nutrients.

INGREDIENTS

hummus
1 large red bell pepper, quartered and seeded
1 (15-ounce) can chickpeas, drained and rinsed
2 tablespoons lemon juice
2 tablespoons tahini
salt and pepper, to taste

4 soft whole-wheat tortillas
1½ cups arugula leaves
½ (14-ounce) can artichoke hearts in oil, drained and quartered

1. Preheat a broiler to high. Put the bell pepper quarters, cut side down, on a broiler pan and broil until the skins are blackened and charred. Put the bell peppers in a plastic bag, seal, and let cool.

2. To make the hummus, remove the skins from the bell peppers and put in a food processor with the chickpeas, lemon juice, and tahini. Process until almost smooth. Season with salt and pepper.

3. Divide the hummus among the tortillas, placing the hummus down the center of the wrap. Top with the arugula and artichoke hearts.

4. Fold the tortilla sides over to enclose the filling and serve immediately.

1   2   3

SOMETHING
DIFFERENT
For a fuller flavor, add ½ teaspoon of crushed red pepper flakes and a crushed garlic clove to the hummus before processing.

Fuller for longer

Extra low sat fat

Whole-Wheat Spaghetti with Edamame

 SERVES 4

PREP TIME:
5 minutes

COOKING TIME:
12–15 minutes

nutritional information per serving	410 cal, 11g fat, 1g sat fat, 3g total sugars, 0.3g salt, 12g fiber, 64g carbs, 18g protein

Edamame (fresh soybeans) are packed with protein, fiber, and vitamins, which can help to reduce cholesterol.

INGREDIENTS

12 ounces whole-wheat spaghetti

1⅓ cups frozen edamame (soybeans)

2 tablespoons extra virgin olive oil

2 garlic cloves, thinly sliced

finely grated rind of 1 lemon

salt and pepper, to taste

1. Bring a saucepan of lightly salted water to a boil over high heat. Add the spaghetti, return to a boil, and cook for 10–12 minutes, or according to the package directions, until tender but still firm to the bite. Add the edamame to the pan for the final 3 minutes of cooking time. Drain the spaghetti and beans well and keep warm in the pan.

2. Meanwhile, put the oil in a small skillet over low heat, stir in the garlic, and heat, stirring occasionally, for about 10 minutes, until the oil picks up the flavor of the garlic; do not let the garlic sizzle or brown.

3. Add the lemon rind, garlic, and oil to the spaghetti and edamame and toss to combine evenly. Season with salt and pepper and serve immediately.

1
2
3

SOMETHING DIFFERENT

Meat eaters may also like to add some thin strips of lean, cooked ham or prosciutto at step 3 with the lemon rind.

Fuller for longer

Extra low sat fat

Super low calorie

Crab Salad Sandwiches

 SERVES 4

PREP TIME:
10 minutes

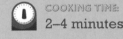 COOKING TIME:
2–4 minutes

nutritional information per serving	300 cal, 10g fat, 1g sat fat, 3g total sugars, 2.3g salt, 6g fiber, 30.5g carbs, 27g protein

This high-taste sandwich is packed with the B vitamins, which will help keep your nervous system healthy.

INGREDIENTS

1 small fennel bulb with leaves

1 pound crabmeat, picked over

2 tablespoons light mayonnaise

2 celery stalks, finely chopped

2 scallions, thinly sliced

1 tablespoon lemon juice

½ teaspoon salt

8 slices whole-wheat bread

1. Remove the leaves from the fennel bulb, then chop and reserve 1 teaspoon of the leaves. Slice the bulb in half lengthwise, then carefully cut each half into paper-thin slices and set aside.

2. In a small bowl, combine the crabmeat, mayonnaise, celery, scallions, fennel leaves, lemon juice, and salt. Stir to mix well.

3. Toast the bread. Divide the crab mixture evenly between four slices of the toasted bread. Top with the paper-thin fennel slices and the remaining four slices of bread. Cut each sandwich in half diagonally and serve immediately.

HEALTHY HINT
To reduce the fat content down even lower, try using fat-free Greek yogurt instead of the mayonnaise.

Falafel Pita Pockets

Fuller for longer

Extra low sat fat

Super low calorie

 SERVES 4

PREP TIME:
15 minutes

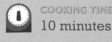 COOKING TIME:
10 minutes

nutritional information per serving	221 cal, 5g fat, 1g sat fat, 5g total sugars, 2g salt, 6g fiber, 35g carbs, 7.6g protein

These filled pita bread contain a variety of nutrients and the chickpeas are high in vitamin E and fiber.

INGREDIENTS

2 garlic cloves

2 tablespoons each of chopped fresh flat-leaf parsley and cilantro

1 teaspoon ground cumin

½ teaspoon salt

1 cup drained and rinsed, canned chickpeas

2 scallions, sliced

2 tablespoons all-purpose flour

1 teaspoon baking powder

1 tablespoon vegetable oil

tzatziki sauce

1 cucumber peeled, seeded, and grated

½ teaspoon salt

⅔ cup low-fat plain yogurt

2 tablespoons lemon juice

2 tablespoons chopped fresh mint leaves

to serve

2 whole-wheat pita breads, halved and warmed

2 tomatoes, diced

2 cups shredded lettuce

1. To make the falafel patties, chop the garlic in a food processor. Add the parsley, cilantro, cumin, and salt and process until the herbs are finely chopped. Add the chickpeas, scallions, flour, and baking powder and process until the texture resembles coarse bread crumbs. Form the falafel mixture into eight patties, about ¼ inch thick.

2. To make the sauce, put the grated cucumber on a double layer of paper towels and sprinkle with half the salt. Set aside. In a medium bowl, combine the yogurt, the remaining salt, lemon juice, and mint and stir to combine. Bundle the cucumber up in the paper towels and, holding over the sink, squeeze out the excess juice. Mix the cucumber into the yogurt mixture. Chill until ready to serve.

3. In a heavy skillet, heat the oil over medium–high heat. When the oil is hot, add the patties and cook for about 3 minutes, or until browned on the bottom. Turn over and cook until browned on the other side. Drain on paper towels.

4. To serve, stuff two falafel patties into each pita half, drizzle with some of the sauce, then add diced tomato and shredded lettuce. Serve immediately.

Extra low sat fat

Super low calorie

Wheat, gluten
& dairy free

Polenta Bruschettas with Tapenade

SERVES 4

PREP TIME:
20 minutes
plus setting

COOKING TIME:
15–20 minutes

nutritional information per serving	280 cal, 20g fat, 3g sat fat, 1.5g total sugars, 0.9g salt, 2g fiber, 19g carbs, 3g protein

Cornmeal-base polenta makes a change from bread in this Italian lunch, and olive oil is one of the healthiest oils.

INGREDIENTS

2 cups boiling water

⅔ cup instant polenta

2 tablespoons olive oil, plus extra for brushing

16 cherry tomatoes on the vine

salt and pepper, to taste

tapenade

½ cup sun-dried tomatoes

½ cup pitted ripe black olives

2 tablespoons capers, rinsed

2 tablespoons chopped fresh flat-leaf parsley

1 garlic clove, crushed

juice of ½ lemon

2 tablespoons extra virgin olive oil

1. Brush a 8½-inch loaf pan with oil. Put the water in a large saucepan with a pinch of salt and bring to a boil.

2. Sprinkle in the polenta and stir continously over moderate heat for about 5 minutes, until thick and smooth. Remove from the heat, stir in the oil, season with salt and pepper, then spread into the prepared pan. Let set.

3. To make the tapenade, finely chop the sun-dried tomatoes, olives, capers, and parsley. Mix with the garlic, lemon juice, and oil, and season with pepper.

4. Preheat the broiler to high. Cut the polenta into eight slices and arrange on a baking sheet with the cherry tomatoes. Brush the polenta with oil and broil until golden, turning once.

5. Serve the polenta slices topped with a spoonful of tapenade and the broiled tomatoes.

**SOMETHING
DIFFERENT**
Try swapping the tomatoes
with vitamin C-rich roasted
red bell pepper quarters.

Fuller for longer

Wheat, gluten
& dairy free

Brown Rice with Asparagus

 SERVES 4

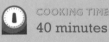 PREP TIME:
10 minutes

COOKING TIME:
40 minutes

nutritional information per serving	468 cal, 20g fat, 4.5g sat fat, 2.5g total sugars, 0.5g salt, 4g fiber, 63g carbs, 9g protein

The unbeatable flavor and texture of fresh green asparagus is perfect for this salad.

INGREDIENTS

1¼ cups brown long-grain rice

1 bay leaf

2½ cups gluten-free vegetable stock or water

8 ounces asparagus, cut into 1¼-inch pieces

juice of 1 lime

2 tablespoons extra virgin olive oil

½ cup coarsely chopped Brazil nuts

salt and pepper, to taste

1. Put the rice and bay leaf in a large saucepan with the stock over high heat and bring to a boil. Stir lightly, then reduce the heat. Cover and simmer, stirring occasionally, for about 35 minutes, or according to the package directions, until all the liquid is absorbed and the rice is just tender. Remove and discard the bay leaf.

2. Meanwhile, bring a saucepan of water to a boil over high heat. Add the asparagus and boil for 3–5 minutes, or until just tender. Alternatively, steam the asparagus for 5–6 minutes over boiling water to preserve more nutrients. Drain well.

3. Combine the rice and asparagus in a large bowl and pour the lime juice and olive oil over the top. Mix well to combine thoroughly.

4. Stir in the Brazil nuts and season with salt and pepper. Serve warm or cold.

1

2

3

COOK'S NOTE
Asparagus is very perishable but will store for two to three days with the cut ends in damp paper towels inside a plastic bag in the refrigerator.

Fuller for longer

Extra low sat fat

Spicy Baked Potatoes

 SERVES 4

 PREP TIME:
15 minutes
plus cooling

COOKING TIME:
1¼–1½ hours

nutritional information per serving	373 cal, 5.5g fat, 0.5g sat fat, 8g total sugars, 0.13g salt, 10g fiber, 70g carbs, 14g protein

Adding spices to your meals increases flavor—and the antioxidant content gets a boost, too.

INGREDIENTS

4 baking potatoes

1 tablespoon vegetable oil (optional)

1 (15-ounce) can chickpeas, drained and rinsed

1 teaspoon ground coriander

1 teaspoon ground cumin

¼ cup chopped fresh cilantro

⅔ cup low-fat plain yogurt

salt and pepper, to taste

salad greens, to serve

1. Preheat the oven to 400°F. Scrub the potatoes and pat them dry with absorbent paper towels. Prick the potatoes all over with a fork, brush with oil, if using, and season with salt and pepper. Put the potatoes on a baking sheet in the preheated oven and bake for 1–1¼ hours, or until cooked through. Cool for 10 minutes.

2. Meanwhile, put the chickpeas in a large mixing bowl and mash with a fork or potato masher. Stir in the ground coriander, cumin, and half the chopped fresh cilantro. Cover the bowl with plastic wrap and set aside.

3. Halve the cooked potatoes and scoop the flesh into a bowl, keeping the shells intact. Mash the flesh until smooth and gently mix into the chickpea mixture with the yogurt. Season with salt and pepper. Place the potato shells on a baking sheet and fill with the potato-and-chickpea mixture. Return the potatoes to the oven and bake for 10–15 minutes, until heated through.

4. Garnish the potatoes with the remaining chopped cilantro and serve with salad greens.

1

2

3

Protein packed

Fuller for longer

Extra low sat fat

Super low calorie

Chicken Tacos

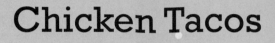

SERVES 4

PREP TIME:
20 minutes

COOKING TIME:
15 minutes

nutritional information per serving	300 cal, 2g fat, 0.5g sat fat, 7.5g total sugars, 1.6g salt, 4g fiber, 43.5g carbs, 29g protein

Salsa is a wonderful way to add fiber and vitamin C to these delicious tacos and is virtually fat free.

INGREDIENTS

salsa
½ red onion, diced

2 jalapeño peppers, seeded and diced

4 tomatoes, diced

2 tablespoons chopped fresh cilantro

3 tablespoons lime juice

½ teaspoon salt

chicken filling
2 teaspoons packed light brown sugar

2 teaspoons ground cumin

1 teaspoon chili powder

½ teaspoon salt

½ teaspoon pepper

1 pound skinless, boneless chicken breasts

8 small corn tortillas, to serve
4 cups shredded lettuce, to serve

1. Make the salsa by putting the onion, jalapeño peppers, and tomatoes into a medium bowl and stirring well. Add the cilantro, lime juice, and salt and stir to combine.

2. To make the chicken filling, preheat the broiler to high or put a ridged grill pan over high heat. In a small bowl, combine the brown sugar, cumin, chili powder, salt, and pepper. Rub the spice mixture all over the chicken breasts. Broil the chicken breasts over high heat for about 4 minutes per side, or until lightly browned on the outside and cooked through with no signs of pink when cut through with a sharp knife. Remove from heat and let cool for about 5 minutes, then slice into ¼-inch thick slices.

3. To serve, heat the tortillas briefly in the broiler, then top with the chicken, salsa, and lettuce. Serve immediately.

Turkey, Mozzarella & Red Pepper Panini

SERVES 4

PREP TIME:
10 minutes
plus cooling

COOKING TIME:
10 minutes

nutritional information per serving	281 cal, 6g fat, 3g sat fat, 10g total sugars, 1g salt, 3.5g fiber, 35g carbs, 23g protein

Rich Mediterranean flavors combine in these irresistible toasted sandwiches, which are surprisingly low in fat.

INGREDIENTS

2 red bell peppers, halved and seeded

4 ciabatta rolls

8 ounces roasted turkey breast, sliced

4 ounces reduced-fat mozzarella, sliced

handful of basil leaves

2 tablespoons sweet chili sauce

1. Preheat the broiler to hot. Put the bell peppers, cut side down, on a broiler pan and cook under the preheated broiler for 4–6 minutes, or until the skins are blackened and charred. Put the peppers in a plastic bag, seal, and let cool. Remove the skins once cool.

2. Slice the rolls open and arrange the turkey on the bottom halves. Top with the mozzarella and basil leaves. Drizzle with chili sauce.

3. Slice the roasted peppers thickly, then arrange over the other ingredients in the rolls.

4. Put a ridged grill pan over high heat and cook the paninis, pressing lightly with a spatula, or put under the preheated hot broiler, until golden. Serve immediately.

1

2

3

SOMETHING DIFFERENT

The paninis can be served untoasted, as crusty sandwich rolls—the filling will be just as delicious.

Extra low sat fat

Super low calorie

Squash & Couscous Salad

 SERVES 4

 PREP TIME: 20 minutes

COOKING TIME: 25 minutes

nutritional information per serving	200 cal, 8.5g fat, 1.1g sat fat, 7g total sugars, 0.14g salt, 3g fiber, 27g carbs, 4g protein

Baking the squash brings out its sweetness in this tasty recipe, which is packed with health-promoting carotenes.

INGREDIENTS

½ butternut squash, seeded, peeled, and cut into small chunks

1 onion, coarsely chopped

1 garlic clove, crushed (optional)

2 tablespoons olive oil

¾ cup couscous

4 sun-dried tomatoes in oil, drained and chopped

1 cup boiling water

3 tablespoons chopped fresh flat-leaf parsley

1 tablespoon lemon juice

salt and pepper, to taste

1. Preheat the oven to 400°F. Put the squash, onion, garlic, if using, and oil in a roasting pan. Toss together. Cover the pan tightly with aluminum foil and bake in the preheated oven for 20–25 minutes, or until the vegetables are just tender. Let stand for 5 minutes before removing the foil.

2. While the vegetables are cooking, put the couscous and sun-dried tomatoes in a heatproof bowl. Pour the boiling water over the grains, then cover the bowl and let stand for 10 minutes, or until all the liquid is absorbed.

3. Fluff up the couscous with a fork. Add the couscous mixture to the vegetables and their juices in the roasting pan with the parsley and lemon juice. Season with salt and pepper, then gently toss together. Serve warm or cold.

1

2

3

HEALTHY HINT

For a gluten-free version, use brown rice instead of couscous; it will also have more fiber and B vitamins.

Extra low sat fat

Super low calorie

Shrimp Rice Noodle Salad

SERVES 4

PREP TIME:
10 minutes

COOKING TIME:
4 minutes

nutritional information per serving	260 cal, 6g fat, 1g sat fat, 3g total sugars, 1g salt, 0.3g fiber, 39g carbs, 10g protein

This refreshing salad is good for a light summer lunch, especially for picnics and lunch boxes.

INGREDIENTS

6 ounces vermicelli rice noodles

8 ounces cooked, peeled shrimp

½ cucumber, cut into matchsticks

1 shallot, thinly sliced

2 tablespoons finely chopped fresh cilantro

dressing
2 tablespoons peanut oil

juice of 1 lime

1 tablespoon sweet chili sauce

1 teaspoon Thai fish sauce

1 teaspoon freshly grated ginger

1. Put the noodles in a bowl, cover with boiling water, and let stand for 4 minutes, or prepare according to the package directions, until tender but firm to the bite. Drain, rinse in cold water, and drain again thoroughly.

2. To make the dressing, put all of the ingredients in a small bowl and beat lightly with a fork to mix.

3. Put the shrimp, cucumber, shallot, and cilantro in a large bowl and stir in the noodles. Pour in the dressing and toss thoroughly with two forks to mix evenly. Serve immediately.

1

2

3

BE PREPARED
This salad will store well for up to 24 hours in the refrigerator if you cover the bowl with plastic wrap.

Protein packed

Fuller for longer

Extra low sat fat

Super low calorie

Thai Crab Cakes

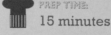 SERVES 6

PREP TIME:
15 minutes

COOKING TIME:
10–15 minutes

nutritional information per serving	114 cal, 4g fat, 0.7g sat fat, 4g total sugars, 0.6g salt, 1g fiber, 8g carbs, 11g protein

This is an ideal lunch for dieters, because the protein and fiber content will help keep you full for hours.

INGREDIENTS

2 cups drained, canned crabmeat

1–2 fresh Thai chiles, seeded and finely chopped

6 scallions, thinly sliced

1¼ cups shredded zucchini

1 cup shredded carrot

1 tablespoon chopped fresh cilantro

2 tablespoons cornstarch

2 egg whites

1 spray sunflower oil

lime wedges, to serve

spicy dipping sauce

⅔ cup low-fat plain yogurt

hot pepper sauce, to taste

2 teaspoons sesame seeds

1. Put the crabmeat in a bowl and stir in the chiles, scallions, zucchini, carrot, and cilantro. Add the cornstarch and mix well.

2. Beat together the egg whites in a separate bowl, then pour into the crab mixture and mix together.

3. Heat a large skillet and lightly spray with the oil, then drop small spoonfuls of the crab mixture into the skillet. Cook the crab cakes over low heat for 3–4 minutes, pressing down with the back of a spatula. Turn over halfway through cooking. Cook the crab cakes in batches.

4. To make the sauce, mix the yogurt and hot pepper sauce in a small bowl and stir in the sesame seeds. Spoon into a small bowl and use as a dipping sauce for the cooked crab cakes. Serve immediately, with lime wedges alongside for squeezing over the cakes.

1

3

4

Stuffed Eggplants

 SERVES 4

PREP TIME:
15 minutes

COOKING TIME:
45 minutes

nutritional information per serving	287 cal, 14g fat, 4.2g sat fat, 9g total sugars, 2.1g salt, 9g fiber, 29g carbs, 12.5g protein

Rich-tasting and satisfying, it's hard to believe these eggplants can easily form part of a low-calorie diet.

INGREDIENTS

2 medium eggplants

1 tablespoon olive oil

1 small onion, diced

2 garlic cloves, finely chopped

¾ cup quinoa

1½ cups vegetable stock

1 teaspoon salt

pinch of pepper

2 tablespoons slivered almonds, toasted

2 tablespoons finely chopped fresh mint, plus extra sprigs to garnish

½ cup crumbled feta cheese

1. Preheat the oven to 450°F. Put the eggplants on a baking sheet and bake for 15 minutes or until soft. Remove from the oven and let cool slightly.

2. Meanwhile, heat the olive oil in a large, heavy skillet over medium–high heat. Add the onion and garlic and cook, stirring occasionally, for about 5 minutes, or until soft. Add the quinoa, stock, salt, and pepper.

3. Cut each eggplant in half lengthwise and scoop out the flesh, leaving a ¼-inch thick border inside the skin so they hold their shape. Chop the flesh and stir it into the quinoa mixture in the skillet. Reduce the heat to medium–low, cover, and cook for about 15 minutes, or until the quinoa is cooked through. Remove from the heat and stir in the almonds, chopped mint, and half of the cheese.

4. Divide the quinoa mixture equally among the eggplant skins and top with the remaining cheese. Bake in the oven for 10–15 minutes, or until the cheese is bubbling and beginning to brown. Garnish with the mint sprigs and serve.

Chicken & Sun-Dried Tomato Pasta *118*

Moroccan-Style Turkey *120*

Roasted Pork with Gingered Apples *122*

Jerk Chicken *124*

Beef Stir-Fry *126*

Pork Meatballs with Tomato Sauce *128*

Chicken & Vegetable Enchiladas *130*

Lean Hamburgers *132*

Chicken Chili *134*

Spanish Rice with Pork & Peppers *136*

Turkey & Cranberry Burgers *138*

Soy & Ginger Pork Tenderloin *140*

Spicy Chicken Skewers *142*

Garlic Chicken with Leeks *144*

Turkey & Oat Meatballs *146*

Shrimp with Ginger *148*

Thai Fish Curry *150*

Broiled Salmon with Mango & Lime Salsa *152*

Fish Tacos with Avocado Salsa *154*

Halibut with Red Pepper & Almond Sauce *156*

Chipotle-Lime Shrimp Burgers *158*

Chunky Monkfish Casserole *160*

Rustic Fish Casserole *162*

Shrimp & Sausage Jambalaya *164*

Meat & Fish Main Dishes

Extra low sat fat

Super low calorie

Chicken & Sun-Dried Tomato Pasta

 SERVES 6

PREP TIME: 25 minutes

COOKING TIME: 15–20 minutes

nutritional information per serving	297 cal, 4g fat, 0.6g sat fat, 1g total sugars, 1.7g salt, 2g fiber, 48.2g carbs, 20g protein

The full flavor of this antioxidant-rich pasta dish belies its tiny fat and saintly low saturates content.

INGREDIENTS

2 cups sun-dried tomatoes (not packed in oil)

12 ounces skinless, boneless chicken breasts, diced

1 teaspoon salt

½ teaspoon pepper

1 spray vegetable oil spray

2 garlic cloves

1½ cups fresh basil, plus leaves to garnish

1 tablespoon olive oil

12 ounces dried pasta

1. Put the tomatoes in a small bowl and cover with boiling water. Let soak for about 20 minutes, until soft, then drain, discarding the soaking liquid.

2. Season the chicken with ½ teaspoon of the salt and the pepper. Coat a large, nonstick skillet with the vegetable oil spray and heat over medium–high heat. Add the chicken and cook, stirring occasionally, for about 5 minutes, or until it is cooked through and just beginning to color. Set aside.

3. Put the rehydrated sun-dried tomatoes in a food processor along with the garlic and basil and process to a paste. Add the oil and the remaining salt and continue to process until smooth.

4. Cook the pasta according to the package directions. Just before draining, scoop out and reserve about ½ cup of the cooking water. Drain the pasta.

5. Toss the hot pasta with the sun-dried tomato pesto, chicken, and as much of the pasta cooking water as needed to make a sauce to coat the pasta. Garnish with basil leaves and serve immediately.

Protein packed

Fuller for longer

Extra low sat fat

Super low calorie

Moroccan-Style Turkey

 SERVES 4

 PREP TIME:
10 minutes

COOKING TIME:
40–45 minutes

nutritional information per serving	254 cal, 2.5g fat, 0.5g sat fat, 7g total sugars, 0.8g salt, 4g fiber, 22g carbs, 28g protein

The chickpeas and apricots in this spiced casserole are a good source of iron for healthy blood.

INGREDIENTS

1 pound skinless, boneless turkey breasts, diced

1 onion, sliced

1 teaspoon ground cumin

½ teaspoon ground cinnamon

1 teaspoon hot chili sauce

1 cup drained and rinsed, canned chickpeas

2½ cups chicken stock

12 dried apricots

⅓ cup cornstarch

⅓ cup cold water

2 tablespoons chopped fresh cilantro

cooked couscous, rice, or baked sweet potatoes, to serve

1. Put the turkey, onion, cumin, cinnamon, chili sauce, chickpeas, and stock into a large saucepan or skillet and bring to a boil. Reduce the heat, cover, and simmer for 15 minutes.

2. Stir in the apricots and return to a boil. Reduce the heat, cover, and simmer for an additional 15 minutes, or until the turkey is thoroughly cooked and tender.

3. Blend the cornstarch with the water in a small bowl and stir into the pan. Return to a boil, stirring continuously, and cook until the mixture thickens. Reduce the heat, cover, and simmer for an additional 5 minutes.

4. Stir half of the cilantro into the turkey mixture. Transfer to a warm serving dish and sprinkle over the remaining cilantro. Serve immediately with cooked couscous, rice, or baked sweet potatoes.

1

2

3

FREEZING TIP
Let cool at the end of Step 3, then put in a container and freeze for up to one month.

Fuller for longer

Extra low sat fat

Super low calorie

Wheat, gluten
& dairy free

Roasted Pork with Gingered Apples

SERVES 4

PREP TIME:
25 minutes plus
marinating

COOKING TIME:
45 minutes

nutritional information per serving	220 cal, 4.5g fat, 1.5g sat fat, 27g total sugars, 0.8g salt, 4g fiber, 25g carbs, 20g protein

Apples make a wonderful, low-calorie change from potatoes in this unusual roasted pork recipe.

INGREDIENTS

2 garlic cloves
¼ cup red wine
2 tablespoons packed light brown sugar
1 tablespoon gluten-free tamari (soy sauce)
1 teaspoon sesame oil
½ teaspoon ground cinnamon
¼ teaspoon ground cloves
1 star anise pod, broken into pieces
½ teaspoon pepper
12 ounces pork tenderloin
steamed green beans, to serve

gingered apples
4 Granny Smith apples, chopped
1 tablespoon rice vinegar
1 tablespoon packed light brown sugar
¼ cup apple juice
1 tablespoon fresh ginger, finely chopped

1. In a bowl large enough to hold the pork, combine the garlic, wine, brown sugar, tamari, sesame oil, cinnamon, cloves, star anise, and pepper. Add the pork and toss to coat. Cover and refrigerate for at least 2 hours or overnight.

2. Preheat the oven to 375°F. Heat a nonstick skillet over high heat. Remove the pork from the marinade, letting any excess run off into the bowl. Cook the pork, turning occasionally, for about 8 minutes, or until browned on all sides.

3. Put the meat in an ovenproof dish and drizzle with a few spoonfuls of the marinade. Roast in the preheated oven for 15 minutes. Turn the meat over, drizzle with more of the marinade, and continue to roast for an additional 30 minutes, or until cooked through (insert the tip of a sharp knife into the center of the meat to check that there is no pink meat).

4. While the meat is roasting, make the gingered apples. In a saucepan, combine the apples, vinegar, sugar, apple juice, and ginger. Cook over medium–high heat, stirring occasionally, until the liquid begins to boil. Reduce the heat to medium–low and simmer, stirring occasionally, for about 20 minutes, or until the apples are soft and the liquid is mostly evaporated.

5. Once the pork has cooked, remove it from the oven and cover the baking dish in a "tent" of aluminum foil. Let the meat rest for about 5 minutes. Slice the meat into ¼-inch thick slices and serve with a spoonful of the gingered apples alongside and the green beans.

Protein packed

Fuller for longer

Extra low sat fat

Super low calorie

Jerk Chicken

SERVES 4

PREP TIME:
10 minutes plus
marinating

COOKING TIME:
30–35 minutes

nutritional information per serving	173 cal, 1.5g fat, 0.5g sat fat, 3g total sugars, 2.2g salt, 0.5g fiber, 3g carbs, 37g protein

Packed with appetite-satisfying chicken and heart-friendly spices, you'll want to cook this again and again.

INGREDIENTS

4 lean chicken pieces

1 bunch scallions, coarsely chopped

1–2 Scotch bonnet chiles, seeded

1 garlic clove

2-inch piece fresh ginger, coarsely chopped

½ teaspoon dried thyme

½ teaspoon paprika

¼ teaspoon ground allspice

pinch ground cinnamon

pinch ground cloves

¼ cup white wine vinegar

3 tablespoons light soy sauce

pepper, to taste

salad greens and crusty bread, to serve

1. Rinse the chicken pieces and pat dry on paper towels. Put them in a shallow dish and make slashes across them with a sharp knife.

2. Put the scallions, chilies, garlic, ginger, thyme, paprika, allspice, cinnamon, cloves, wine vinegar, soy sauce in a food processor, season with pepper, and process until smooth.

3. Pour the spicy mixture over the chicken. Turn the chicken pieces over so that they are well coated in the marinade.

4. Transfer the chicken pieces to the refrigerator and let marinate for up to 24 hours.

5. Preheat the broiler to medium. Remove the chicken from the marinade and broil for about 30–35 minutes, turning the chicken over and basting occasionally with any remaining marinade. Broil until the chicken is cooked through, so that when the tip of a sharp knife is inserted into the thickest part of the meat, the juices run clear with no traces of pink. Transfer the chicken to individual serving plates and serve immediately with salad greens and crusty bread.

Beef Stir-Fry

Low on carbs

Protein packed

Extra low sat fat

Super low calorie

SERVES 4

PREP TIME:
10 minutes

COOKING TIME:
10–12 minutes

nutritional information per serving	80 cal, 1.5g fat, 0.5g sat fat, 4g total sugars, 0.4g salt, 2.5g fiber, 4.5g carbs, 10g protein

Lean beef is extremely high in iron, and bell peppers are rich in vitamin C, which helps you absorb that iron.

INGREDIENTS

2–3 sprays olive oil spray

5 ounces bottom round roast or rump roast beef, cut into thin strips

1 orange bell pepper, seeded and cut into thin strips

4 scallions, chopped

1–2 fresh jalapeño peppers, seeded and chopped

2–3 garlic cloves, chopped

2 cups trimmed and diagonally halved snow peas

4 ounces large portobello mushrooms, sliced

1–2 teaspoons hoisin sauce

1 tablespoon orange juice

3 cups arugula

1. Preheat a wok or large skillet, then spray in the oil and heat for 30 seconds. Add the beef and stir-fry for 1 minute, or until browned. Using a slotted spoon, remove and reserve.

2. Add the orange bell pepper, scallions, jalapeño peppers, and garlic and stir-fry for 2 minutes. Add the snow peas and mushrooms and stir-fry for an additional 2 minutes.

3. Return the beef to the wok and add the hoisin sauce and orange juice. Stir-fry for 2–3 minutes, or until the beef is tender and the vegetables are tender but still firm to the bite. Stir in the arugula and stir-fry until it starts to wilt. Serve immediately.

GOES WELL WITH *Serve with brown rice or whole-wheat noodles to boost fiber.*

Fuller for longer

Extra low sat fat

Pork Meatballs with Tomato Sauce

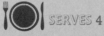

SERVES 4

PREP TIME:
15 minutes

COOKING TIME:
40–45 minutes

nutritional information per serving	463 cal, 10g fat, 1.5g sat fat, 10g total sugars, 0.6g salt, 6g fiber, 58g carbs, 40g protein

Lean pork is much lower in fat than many people think and is high in various minerals and the B vitamins.

INGREDIENTS

1 pound lean pork tenderloin

4 reduced-fat link pork sausages, skins removed and coarsely chopped

3–4 teaspoons canola oil or sunflower oil

1 onion, finely chopped

1 (28-ounce) can diced tomatoes

⅔ cup chicken or vegetable stock

1 carrot, finely chopped

1 celery stalk, finely chopped

1 teaspoon dried oregano

8 ounces dried spaghetti

salt and pepper, to taste

1. Put the pork tenderloin in a food processor and process until finely chopped. Transfer to a bowl. Add the sausagemeat and mix well, then roll into 20 walnut-size balls.

2. Heat 2 teaspoons of oil in a large saucepan. Add the onion, cover, and cook over low heat for 2–3 minutes, or until softened. Stir in the tomatoes, stock, carrot, celery, and oregano. Simmer, uncovered, for 15–20 minutes, or until the sauce has reduced and thickened slightly.

3. Meanwhile, heat 1 teaspoon of oil in a large skillet. Add the meatballs, in batches, and cook for 2–3 minutes, adding a little extra oil, if necessary, and turning several times, until well browned all over. Transfer to a plate with a slotted spoon.

4. Season the sauce with salt and pepper. Add the meatballs, then cover the skillet and simmer for 8–10 minutes, or until cooked through. Cook the spaghetti in a large saucepan of boiling, lightly salted water according to the package directions, until tender but still firm to the bite. Drain and return to the hot pan. Add the meatballs and sauce and toss well to mix. Serve immediately.

Fuller for longer

Extra low sat fat

Super low calorie

Chicken & Vegetable Enchiladas

 SERVES 4

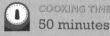 PREP TIME:
20 minutes

COOKING TIME:
50 minutes

nutritional information per serving	296 cal, 7.5g fat, 3g sat fat, 5g total sugars, 2g salt, 4g fiber, 35g carbs, 25g protein

These enchiladas are packed with the plant compound lycopene, which protects against cancer and heart disease.

INGREDIENTS

2 sprays olive oil spray

2 zucchini, diced

1 red bell pepper, seeded and diced

1 teaspoon salt

1 onion, diced

2 garlic cloves, finely chopped

1 tablespoon chili powder

1 tablespoon dried oregano

¾ cup tomato puree or tomato sauce

1 cup vegetable stock

1¼ cups shredded, cooked chicken breast

8 small corn tortillas

½ cup shredded reduced-fat cheddar cheese

1. Preheat the oven to 450°F. Spray a large, rimmed baking sheet with half a spray of olive oil spray.

2. Spread the zucchini and bell pepper on the prepared baking sheet and spray with half a spray of olive oil spray. Sprinkle with half of the salt. Bake in the preheated oven for about 20 minutes, or until soft and beginning to brown.

3. Meanwhile, spray a large skillet with 1 spray of olive oil and put over medium–high heat. Add the onion and garlic and cook, stirring, for about 5 minutes, or until soft. Add the chili powder and oregano and cook for an additional minute. Add the tomato puree or sauce and stock and bring to a boil. Reduce the heat to medium and simmer, stirring occasionally, for 5 minutes. Stir in the remaining salt. Puree the sauce, in batches, in a blender or food processor, or use a handheld immersion blender.

4. When the vegetables are done, remove them from the oven and reduce the heat to 350°F. In a large bowl, combine the vegetables, shredded chicken, and several spoonfuls of the sauce. Stir well.

5. Coat the bottom of a 9 x 13-inch baking dish with a thin layer of the sauce. Put four of the tortillas on the bottom of the dish, overlapping as little as possible. Top the tortillas with the chicken-vegetable mixture and then a second layer of four tortillas. Top the stacks with the remaining sauce, then sprinkle the cheese over the top.

6. Bake in the preheated oven for about 30 minutes, until the enchiladas are heated through and the cheese is bubbling and beginning to color. Serve immediately.

Fuller for longer

Extra low sat fat

Super low calorie

Lean Hamburgers

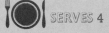 SERVES 4

PREP TIME:
15 minutes
plus chilling

COOKING TIME:
25–30 minutes

nutritional information per serving	116 cal, 5g fat, 2g sat fat, 6g total sugars, 0.2g salt, 2.5g fiber, 7g carbs, 11g protein

Everyone loves a tasty hamburger and, cooked our way, it really is good for you.

INGREDIENTS

6 ounces fresh, lean ground beef

2 shallots, finely chopped

1 tablespoon Worcestershire sauce, or to taste

2 sprays sunflower oil spray

2 onions, thinly sliced

4 beefsteak tomatoes

1–2 garlic cloves

pepper, to taste

ketchup, to serve (optional)

mixed salad greens, to serve

1. Put the ground beef in a bowl, add the shallots and Worcestershire sauce, and season with pepper. Mix together and, with damp hands, shape into four equal patties. Put the patties on a plate, cover lightly with plastic wrap, and chill in the refrigerator until required.

2. Heat a large skillet, spray with the oil, and add the sliced onions. Cook over low heat for 12–15 minutes, stirring frequently, until the onions are tender. Keep warm if necessary. Preheat the broiler to high and line the broil rack with aluminum foil.

3. Cut the tomatoes into thick slices and the garlic cloves into slivers. Stud the tomatoes with the garlic and put on the broiler rack together with the patties.

4. Cook the patties for 3–4 minutes on each side, or according to personal preference. If the tomatoes are cooking too quickly, either remove them and add a little later or remove and keep warm. Serve each burger between the thick tomato slices with the onion garnish, ketchup, if using, and salad greens.

Low on carbs

Protein packed

Fuller for longer

Extra low sat fat

Super low calorie

Wheat, gluten
& dairy free

Chicken Chili

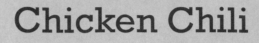

SERVES 6

PREP TIME:
10 minutes

COOKING TIME:
35–40 minutes

nutritional information per serving	219 cal, 5.5g fat, 1g sat fat, 4g total sugars, 1.1g salt, 4g fiber, 10g carbs, 26g protein

Cannellini beans area a rich source of protein and are filling so there's no need to add rice to this chili.

INGREDIENTS

1 tablespoon vegetable oil

1 onion, diced

2 garlic cloves, finely chopped

1 green bell pepper, seeded and diced

1 small jalapeño pepper, seeded and diced

2 teaspoons chili powder

2 teaspoons dried oregano

1 teaspoon ground cumin

1 teaspoon salt

2 cups drained and rinsed, canned cannellini beans

3 cups gluten-free chicken stock

1 pound cooked chicken breasts, shredded

juice of 1 lime

⅔ cup chopped cilantro, plus leaves to garnish

1. Heat the oil in a large, heavy saucepan over medium–high heat. Add the onion, garlic, bell pepper, and jalapeño and cook, stirring occasionally, for about 5 minutes, or until soft. Add the chili powder, oregano, cumin, and salt and cook, stirring, for about an additional 30 seconds.

2. Add the beans and stock and bring to a boil. Reduce the heat to medium–low and simmer gently, uncovered, for about 20 minutes.

3. Ladle about half of the bean mixture into a blender or food processor and puree. Return the puree to the pan along with the shredded chicken. Simmer for about 10 minutes or until heated through. Just before serving, stir in the lime juice and cilantro. Garnish with cilantro leaves and serve immediately.

Spanish Rice with Pork & Red Peppers

 SERVES 1

PREP TIME:
10 minutes

COOKING TIME:
45–55 minutes

nutritional information per serving	476 cal, 7g fat, 2g sat fat, 19g total sugars, 0.9g salt, 8g fiber, 65g carbs, 25g protein

A colorful taste of Spain but with a healthy twist, the brown rice boosts the fiber and vitamin-B content.

INGREDIENTS

½ teaspoon olive oil

3 ounces lean pork tenderloin, cut into small cubes

1 small onion, or 2 shallots, finely chopped

1 garlic clove, chopped

1 red or orange bell pepper, seeded and chopped into ½-inch cubes

¾ cup canned diced tomatoes

1 tablespoon chopped fresh parsley

pinch of saffron strands

⅓ cup brown long-grain rice

1 cup chicken or vegetable stock

pepper, to taste

1. Heat the oil in a large, heavy, lidded saucepan and brown the pork on all sides on high heat. Remove with a slotted spoon and keep warm.

2. Reduce the heat to medium–high, add the onion, garlic, and bell pepper, and stir-fry for a few minutes, until everything is soft and turning golden.

3. Return the meat to the pan and add the tomatoes, parsley, saffron, rice, and stock, and season with pepper. Stir well to combine and to break up the tomatoes a little, and bring to a simmer. Turn the heat down to low and put the lid on.

4. Simmer for 30–40 minutes, or until the rice is tender and all the stock is absorbed. (If the rice is not cooked but the dish looks dry, add a little more hot water.) Remove from the heat and serve.

1

2

3

SOMETHING DIFFERENT
Skinless, boneless chicken thighs make a great subsitute for the pork and are similarly rich in the B vitamins and minerals.

Protein packed

Fuller for longer

Extra low sat fat

Super low calorie

Turkey & Cranberry Burgers

 SERVES 4

 PREP TIME:
10 minutes
plus chilling

COOKING TIME:
30 minutes

nutritional information per serving	247 cal, 3.5g fat, 0.6g sat fat, 8g total sugars, 0.7g salt, 2g fiber, 24g carbs, 29g protein

The perfect healthy way to use up leftover turkey, our dinner is simple to make and delicious, too.

INGREDIENTS

12 ounces lean ground turkey

1 onion, finely chopped

1 tablespoon chopped fresh sage

⅓ cup dry white bread crumbs

¼ cup cranberry sauce

1 egg white, lightly beaten

2 teaspoons sunflower oil, for brushing

salt and pepper, to taste

to serve

4 toasted whole-grain or whole-wheat burger buns

½ lettuce, shredded

4 tomatoes, sliced

4 teaspoons cranberry sauce

1. Mix together the turkey, onion, sage, seasoning, bread crumbs, and cranberry sauce in a large bowl, then bind with egg white.

2. Press into four 4-inch patties, about ¾ inch thick. Chill the patties in the refrigerator for 30 minutes.

3. Preheat the broiler to medium and line the broiler rack with aluminum foil. Place the patties on top and brush lightly with oil. Put under the preheated broiler and cook for 10 minutes. Turn the burgers over and brush again with oil. Cook for an additional 12–15 minutes, or until cooked through.

4. Fill the burger buns with lettuce, tomato, and a burger, and top with cranberry sauce.

1

2

4

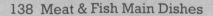

HEALTHY HINT
For an even lower-calorie meal, serve the burger on half a bun, as an open sandwich.

Low on carbs

Protein packed

Fuller for longer

Extra low sat fat

Super low calorie

Soy & Ginger Pork Tenderloin

 SERVES 4   PREP TIME: 10–15 minutes   COOKING TIME: 40 minutes

nutritional information per serving	220 cal, 7.5g fat, 2g sat fat, 6g total sugars, 1g salt, 3g fiber, 6g carbs, 31g protein

A Chinese-style dish that uses a low-fat cut of pork in a richly flavored sauce.

INGREDIENTS

2 teaspoons sunflower oil

1 pound lean pork tenderloin

4 shallots, thinly sliced

2 teaspoons soy sauce

1 garlic clove, crushed

1 tablespoon honey

1-inch piece grated fresh ginger

⅔ cup chicken stock

3½ cups closed-cup mushrooms, sliced

1 small bok choy, quartered

salt and pepper, to taste

1. Put a wide, heavy skillet or flameproof casserole dish over high heat. Meanwhile, brush the oil over the surface of the pork.

2. Put the pork in the hot skillet and cook, turning occasionally, for about 10 minutes, or until golden brown on all sides. Add the shallots to the skillet and sauté for 1 minute, stirring continuously.

3. Mix together the soy sauce, garlic, honey, and ginger in a small bowl. Spread the soy mixture evenly over the pork in the skillet.

4. Pour the stock into the skillet and bring to a boil. Reduce the heat to low and simmer gently for about 20 minutes, turning the pork occasionally in the juices. Remove the pork from the skillet with a slotted spoon and let rest on a warm dish. Check that the pork is cooked through, with no traces of pink, and that the juices run clear when you cut into the meat.

5. Add the mushrooms and bok choy to the skillet and increase the heat until boiling. Reduce the heat and simmer for 4–5 minutes, or until tender. Season with salt and pepper. Slice the pork diagonally, adding the juices back to the skillet.

6. Serve the sliced pork on top of the vegetables, with the juices spooned over the top.

Spicy Chicken Skewers

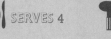 SERVES 4

PREP TIME:
15 minutes
plus soaking

COOKING TIME:
8–10 minutes

nutritional information per serving	186 cal, 2g fat, 0.5g sat fat, 12g total sugars, 0.5g salt, 1g fiber, 12g carbs, 31g protein

A simple, quick, and easy dinner that is ideal for dieters watching their calories or fat intake.

INGREDIENTS

1 pound skinless, boneless chicken breasts

3 tablespoons tomato paste

2 tablespoons honey

2 tablespoons Worcestershire sauce

1 tablespoon chopped fresh rosemary

16 cherry tomatoes

fresh rosemary sprigs, to garnish

freshly cooked couscous or rice, to serve

1. Using a sharp knife, cut the chicken into 1-inch chunks and put in a bowl. Mix together the tomato paste, honey, Worcestershire sauce, and rosemary in a separate bowl, then add to the chicken, stirring to coat evenly.

2. Soak eight wooden skewers in a bowl of cold water for 30 minutes to prevent them from burning during cooking. Preheat the broiler to hot. Thread the chicken pieces and cherry tomatoes alternately onto the skewers and put them on a broiler rack.

3. Spoon over any remaining glaze and cook under the preheated broiler for 8–10 minutes, turning occasionally, until the chicken is cooked through. Transfer to four large serving plates, garnish with a few sprigs of fresh rosemary, and serve with freshly cooked couscous or rice.

HEALTHY HINT

To keep the calorie content low, serve just 2 tablespoons couscous and add a green salad.

Garlic Chicken with Leeks

Low on carbs

Protein packed

Fuller for longer

Extra low sat fat

Super low calorie

 SERVES 4

PREP TIME: 10 minutes

COOKING TIME: 8–10 minutes

nutritional information per serving	206 cal, 5g fat, 1g sat fat, 9.5g total sugars, 1.5g salt, 2.5g fiber, 9.5g carbs, 28.5g protein

Chicken and leeks always taste great together and combine well with the unmistakable flavor of fresh ginger and soy sauce.

INGREDIENTS

1 pound skinless, boneless chicken breasts, finely chopped
1 tablespoon peanut oil
6 garlic cloves, thinly sliced
1-inch piece finely grated fresh ginger
3 leeks, thinly sliced
4 scallions, chopped
1 tablespoon honey

marinade
2 tablespoons rice wine
2 tablespoons dark soy sauce
1 teaspoon sesame oil

1. To make the marinade, put the rice wine, soy sauce, and sesame oil in a large mixing bowl. Add the chicken pieces and mix together.

2. Drain the chicken, reserving the marinade. Preheat a wok or large skillet over high heat. Add the oil and heat until hot. Add the drained chicken and stir-fry for 3 minutes to seal.

3. Add the garlic, ginger, leeks, and scallions to the wok and sauté for 3 minutes to soften. Add the reserved marinade and honey and stir-fry for an additional minute, until the chicken is cooked through.

4. Transfer to warm serving bowls and serve immediately.

1

2

3

Serve with cooked rice or noodles that can be softened by submerging in boiling water.

Turkey & Oat Meatballs

 SERVES 4

🍴 PREP TIME:
15 minutes plus
soaking and chilling

⏲ COOKING TIME:
10–12 minutes

nutritional information per serving	191 cal, 4g fat, 1g sat fat, 4.5g total sugars, 0.2g salt, 2.5g fiber, 15g carbs, 23g protein

Light and simple meat skewers are winners for summer barbecues, especially when served with a colorful salad.

INGREDIENTS

8 ounces ground turkey
¾ cup rolled oats
4 scallions, finely chopped
1½ tablespoons chopped fresh thyme
1 egg white
olive oil, for brushing
salt and pepper, to taste
paprika, to sprinkle
mixed greens, to serve

sauce
⅔ cup low-fat plain yogurt
1 garlic clove, crushed
¼ cucumber, shredded

1. Presoak eight wooden skewers in cold water for about 30 minutes.

2. Put the turkey, oats, scallions, thyme, and egg white in a bowl and season with salt and pepper. Mix with your hands until evenly combined. Divide the mixture into eight even pieces and shape into ovals around the prepared skewers. Let chill in the refrigerator for an hour.

3. Preheat a broiler or barbecue to high. Brush the meatballs lightly with oil and place under the hot broiler, turning occasionally, for 10–12 minutes, or until golden brown and thoroughly cooked.

4. Meanwhile, make the sauce. Mix together the yogurt, garlic, and cucumber in a small bowl. Sprinkle the meatball skewers with paprika and serve hot, with the sauce and a mixed salad on the side.

2

2

4

FREEZING TIP
Prepare up to the
end of step 2,
then freeze until
firm. Pack in
an airtight
container and
freeze for up
to two months.
Thaw thoroughly
before cooking.

Shrimp with Ginger

Protein packed

Fuller for longer

Extra low sat fat

Super low calorie

Wheat, gluten & dairy free

SERVES 4

PREP TIME:
10 minutes

COOKING TIME:
25–30 minutes

nutritional information per serving	180 cal, 9g fat, 1.5g sat fat, 7.5g total sugars, 2.4g salt, 3g fiber, 10g carbs, 22g protein

Selenium- and zinc-rich shrimp and plant compounds in the ginger give this dish huge immune-boosting powers.

INGREDIENTS

1 teaspoon chopped fresh ginger

1 teaspoon crushed fresh garlic

1 teaspoon salt

1 teaspoon chili powder

2 tablespoons lemon juice

3 tablespoons oil

3 onions, chopped

1 green bell pepper, sliced

1 (14½-ounce) can diced tomatoes

12 ounces cooked, peeled shrimp

fresh cilantro leaves, to garnish

boiled rice, to serve

1. Put the ginger, garlic, salt, and chili powder in a small bowl and mix to combine. Add the lemon juice and mix to form a paste.

2. Heat the oil in a saucepan. Add the onions and green bell pepper and sauté until browned.

3. Add the spice paste to the onions, reduce the heat to low, and cook, stirring and mixing well, for about 3 minutes. Add the tomatoes and cook for 5–7 minutes, stirring occasionally.

4. Add the shrimp to the pan and cook for 10 minutes, stirring occasionally. Garnish with fresh cilantro and serve with rice.

COOK'S NOTE

Chop your garlic and ginger just before using to retain more of their nutrients and flavor.

Thai Fish Curry

Low on carbs

Protein packed

Fuller for longer

Super low calorie

Wheat, gluten & dairy free

SERVES 4

PREP TIME:
10 minutes

COOKING TIME:
20–25 minutes

nutritional information per serving	248 cal, 8.5g fat, 4g sat fat, 0.9g total sugars, 0.3g salt, 0.5g fiber, 1.1g carbs, 42g protein

Here's an easy yet delicious way to enjoy white fish— the Thai spices add plenty of flavor without calories.

INGREDIENTS

1 tablespoon oil

2 scallions, sliced

1 teaspoon cumin seeds, ground

2 fresh green chiles, chopped

1 teaspoon coriander seeds, ground

⅛ cup chopped fresh cilantro

1 teaspoon chopped fresh mint

1 tablespoon snipped fresh chives

⅔ cup light coconut milk

4 white fish fillets, about 8 ounces each

salt and pepper, to taste

1 teaspoon chopped fresh mint, to garnish

cooked long-grain rice, to serve

1. Heat the oil in a large skillet or shallow saucepan and add the scallions. Sauté the scallions over medium heat until they are softened but not browned.

2. Stir in the cumin, chiles, and ground coriander, and cook until fragrant. Add the fresh cilantro, mint, chives, and coconut milk and season with salt and pepper.

3. Carefully place the fish fillets in the skillet and poach for 10–15 minutes, or until the flesh flakes when tested with a fork.

4. Garnish the curry with the chopped mint and serve immediately, with the long-grain rice on the side.

1

2

3

HEALTHY HINT
Peanut oil, with
its good balance
of healthy fats,
is the ideal oil
to use in this
recipe.

Low on carbs

Fuller for longer

Super low calorie

Wheat, gluten
& dairy free

Broiled Salmon with Mango & Lime Salsa

SERVES 4

PREP TIME:
15 minutes

COOKING TIME:
8–10 minutes

nutritional information
per serving

290 cal, 17.5g fat, 6g sat fat, 9g total sugars, 0.1g salt,
3g fiber, 10g carbs, 24g protein

The refreshing, clean flavors of mango and lime are good with oily fish, such as salmon.

INGREDIENTS

2 tablespoons lime juice

1 tablespoon honey

1 tablespoon chopped fresh dill

4 salmon fillets, about 4 ounces each

salt and pepper, to taste

boiled new potatoes and salad greens, to serve (optional)

salsa

1 ripe mango, peeled, pitted, and diced

finely grated rind and juice of 1 lime

2 tablespoons dried coconut

1 tablespoon chopped fresh dill

1. Preheat the broiler to high and lay a piece of aluminum foil on the broiler rack. Mix together the lime juice, honey, and dill in a wide dish. Season with salt and pepper.

2. Put the salmon fillets in the dish and turn to coat evenly in the glaze. Arrange on the prepared broiler rack and broil for 4–5 minutes on each side, turning once, or until cooked through.

3. Meanwhile, prepare the salsa. Mix the mango in a small bowl with the lime rind and juice. Stir in the coconut and dill.

4. Serve the salmon hot, with the salsa spooned over the top and new potatoes and salad greens alongside, if desired.

1

2

3

COOK'S NOTE
Prick a fresh
lime and
microwave it
on high for
30 seconds to
get a lot more
juice from it.

Fuller for longer

Extra low sat fat

Super low calorie

Fish Tacos with Avocado Salsa

SERVES 4

PREP TIME:
15 minutes

COOKING TIME:
5–10 minutes

nutritional information per serving	300 cal, 14g fat, 1g sat fat, 3g total sugars, 1.3g salt, 3.5g fiber, 22g carbs, 22g protein

The warm and inviting tastes of Mexico make this quick, high-nutrient dinner a real treat.

INGREDIENTS

salsa
½ red onion, diced
2 jalapeño peppers, seeded and diced
2 tomatoes, diced
½ avocado, diced
2 tablespoons chopped fresh cilantro
3 tablespoons lime juice
½ teaspoon salt

fish
2 tablespoons lime juice
1 tablespoon olive oil
1 teaspoon ground cumin
1 teaspoon chili powder
½ teaspoon salt
1 pound white fish fillets

to serve
8 small corn tortillas
3 cups shredded red cabbage

1. Put all the salsa ingredients in a medium bowl and stir to mix well.

2. Preheat the broiler to medium–high or put a ridged grill pan over medium–high heat. In a small bowl, combine the lime juice, olive oil, cumin, chili powder, and salt.

3. Brush the lime mixture on both sides of the fish fillets. Broil the fish over medium–high heat for about 2–4 minutes per side, or until striped marks start to appear and the fish is opaque and cooked through. Chop the fish into bite-size chunks.

4. To serve, warm the tortillas under the broiler, then top them with the fish, salsa, and shredded cabbage. Roll up and serve immediately.

Low on carbs

Protein packed

Fuller for longer

Extra low sat fat

Super low calorie

Halibut with
Red Pepper & Almond Sauce

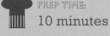 SERVES 4   PREP TIME: 10 minutes   COOKING TIME: 15 minutes

nutritional information **per serving**	261 cal, 7g fat, 1g sat fat, 4.5g total sugars, 1.4g salt, 1.7g fiber, 10g carbs, 40g protein

High in protein, low in fat, and with a fine flavor, halibut balances well with a rich Mediterranean sauce.

INGREDIENTS

1½ pounds halibut fillets
¾ teaspoon salt
½ teaspoon pepper
green vegetables, to serve

sauce

1 large red bell pepper
3 garlic cloves, with skins
¼ cup slivered, toasted almonds
1 thick slice of bread, torn into a few pieces
1 teaspoon salt
1 teaspoon paprika
1 cup canned diced tomatoes
2 tablespoons red wine vinegar

1. To make the sauce, preheat the broiler. Quarter the bell pepper and put the pieces, cut side down, on a baking sheet along with the garlic cloves. Broil, turning the garlic cloves once, until the cloves are browned and soft and the skin of the bell pepper blackens and blisters. Remove from the broiler and set aside to cool slightly.

2. When cool enough to handle, peel the blackened skin from the bell pepper and remove the core and seeds, discarding both. Push the garlic flesh out of the skins. Put the roasted pepper and garlic in a food processor along with the almonds, bread, salt, and paprika. Process to a paste. Add the tomatoes and vinegar and process until the tomatoes are smooth and completely incorporated.

3. To cook the fish, preheat a broiler to high or heat a ridged grill pan over high heat. Season the fish with salt and pepper and broil for about 4 minutes. Turn and broil on the second side for an additional 4 minutes or until the fish is opaque and cooked through. Serve the fish immediately, with the sauce drizzled over it and green vegetables.

GOES WELL WITH

This goes well with a portion of unpeeled, steamed new potatoes, garnished with a drizzle of olive oil.

Protein packed

Fuller for longer

Extra low sat fat

Super low calorie

Chipotle-Lime Shrimp Burgers

 SERVES 4

PREP TIME:
10–15 minutes

COOKING TIME:
6–8 minutes

nutritional information per serving	300 cal, 7.5g fat, 1.1g sat fat, 2g total sugars, 3.3g salt, 3.5g fiber, 31g carbs, 31g protein

This light burger makes a fantastic change from meat-base ones and is low in saturated fat.

INGREDIENTS

1¼ pounds cooked, peeled shrimp

1 celery stalk, finely diced

2 scallions, finely chopped

2 tablespoons finely chopped fresh cilantro

1 garlic clove, finely chopped

½ teaspoon salt

½ teaspoon ground chipotle

zest and juice of 1 lime

2 teaspoons olive oil

2 tablespoons light mayonnaise

4 small whole-wheat burger buns, toasted

4 lettuce leaves

1. Process 1 pound of the shrimp in a food processor. Dice the remaining shrimp. In a medium bowl, combine the pureed and diced shrimp. Add the celery, scallions, cilantro, garlic, salt, ground chipotle, and lime zest and juice and mix well.

2. Form the shrimp mixture into four patties. Heat the oil in a large skillet over medium–high heat. Add the shrimp patties and cook for about 3–4 minutes or until browned underneath. Flip the patties over and cook for an additional 3–4 minutes, or until browned and cooked through.

3. Spread the mayonnaise onto the lower halves of the buns, dividing evenly. Place one shrimp burger on the lower half of each bun, then top with a lettuce leaf and the top half of the bun. Serve immediately.

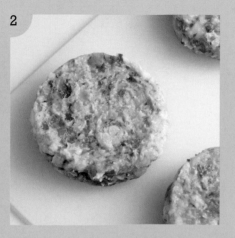

COOK'S NOTE
Chipotle is a smoked
dried jalapeño pepper—
if you can't get it, use
smoked paprika instead.

Protein packed

Fuller for longer

Extra low sat fat

Super low calorie

Chunky Monkfish Casserole

 SERVES 4

PREP TIME:
10 minutes

 COOKING TIME:
20–25 minutes

nutritional information per serving	250 cal, 7g fat, 1g sat fat, 7g total sugars, 0.5g salt, 3g fiber, 16g carbs, 27g protein

Colorful and flavorful, this seafood casserole cooks in record time, perfect for easy and informal entertaining.

INGREDIENTS

2 tablespoons olive oil

1 onion, thinly sliced

1 large yellow bell pepper, seeded and thinly sliced

1 celery stalk, sliced

1¼ cups fish stock

1 (14½-ounce) can diced tomatoes

1⅓ cups fresh or canned corn kernels

1 pound monkfish fillet, cut into chunks

8 peeled and deveined, raw jumbo shrimp

salt and pepper, to taste

gremolata

finely grated rind of 1 lemon

2 tablespoons finely chopped fresh flat-leaf parsley

1 garlic clove, finely chopped

1. Heat the oil in a large, flameproof casserole dish over medium heat and sauté the onion, bell pepper, and celery, stirring occasionally, for about 10 minutes, or until softened but not brown.

2. Add the fish stock and tomatoes and bring to a boil. Stir in the corn kernels and season with salt and pepper, then add the chunks of monkfish and bring back to a boil. Put the shrimp on top.

3. Reduce the heat to low and let simmer gently for about 10 minutes, or until the fish is firm and the shrimp have turned pink.

4. Meanwhile, prepare the gremolata by mixing together the lemon rind, parsley, and garlic in a small bowl.

5. Sprinkle the gremolata over the casserole and serve immediately.

Rustic Fish Casserole

Low on carbs

Protein packed

Fuller for longer

Extra low sat fat

Super low calorie

 SERVES 4

PREP TIME:
10 minutes

COOKING TIME:
10–15 minutes

nutritional information per serving	230 cal, 8g fat, 1g sat fat, 6g total sugars, 1.4g salt, 2.8g fiber, 8g carbs, 30.5g protein

A bowl of steaming fish stew with crusty bread is a meal that is quick and easy to rustle up.

INGREDIENTS

12 ounces live clams, scrubbed

2 tablespoons olive oil

1 large onion, chopped

2 garlic cloves, crushed

2 celery stalks, sliced

12 ounces firm white fish fillet

8 ounces prepared squid rings

1¾ cups fish stock

6 plum tomatoes, chopped

small bunch of fresh thyme

salt and pepper, to taste

crusty bread, to serve

1. Discard any clams with broken shells and any that refuse to close when tapped.

2. Heat the oil in a large skillet over medium heat. Add the onion, garlic, and celery and cook, stirring occasionally, for 3–4 minutes, until softened but not browned. Meanwhile, cut the fish into chunks.

3. Stir the fish and squid into the skillet, then cook gently for 2 minutes. Stir in the stock, tomatoes, and thyme and season with salt and pepper. Cover and simmer gently for 3–4 minutes. Add the clams, cover, and cook over high heat for an additional 2 minutes, or until the shells open. Discard any that remain closed.

4. Transfer to warm serving bowls and serve immediately with crusty bread.

2   3   3

SOMETHING
DIFFERENT
Try mussels instead
of clams for a change.
For the white fish,
monkfish, halibut, red
snapper, and sea bass
are all ideal.

Extra low sat fat

Super low calorie

Shrimp & Sausage Jambalaya

🍴|🍽️ SERVES 6   👨‍🍳 PREP TIME: 10 minutes   ⏱️ COOKING TIME: 40–45 minutes

nutritional information per serving	270 cal, 6g fat, 2g sat fat, 5g total sugars, 1.8g salt, 2g fiber, 27g carbs, 20g protein

Shrimp and spicy sausage are a heavenly combination, and this dish is low in both fat and calories.

INGREDIENTS

1 tablespoon olive oil

1 onion, diced

2 garlic cloves, finely chopped

1 green bell pepper, seeded and diced

2 celery stalks, diced

1 cup long-grain white rice

1 tablespoon paprika

2 teaspoons dried oregano

2 teaspoons dried thyme

1 teaspoon salt

½ teaspoon cayenne pepper, or to taste

½ teaspoon pepper

1 (14½-ounce) can diced tomatoes

3 cups chicken stock

1 bay leaf

4 ounces diced Andouille sausage or spicy Italian sausage, cooked and diced

1 pound cooked, peeled shrimp

1. Heat the oil in a large, heavy saucepan over medium–high heat. Add the onion, garlic, green bell pepper, and celery and cook, stirring occasionally, for about 5 minutes, or until soft.

2. Add the rice, paprika, oregano, thyme, salt, cayenne, and pepper and cook for about an additional 30 seconds. Add the tomatoes, stock, and bay leaf. Reduce the heat to medium, cover, and cook, stirring occasionally, for about 25–30 minutes, or until the rice is tender.

3. Stir in the sausage and then add the shrimp and cook, uncovered, for about 6–8 minutes, or until the sausage and shrimp are warmed through. Remove and discard the bay leaf. Serve immediately.

Sweet & Sour Noodles *168*

Spicy Black-Eyed Peas *170*

Butternut Squash & Lentil Stew *172*

Spicy Ciabatta Pizza *174*

Bean Burgers *176*

Spicy Corn Chowder *178*

Tofu Steak with Fennel & Orange *180*

Stuffed Tomatoes *182*

Broccoli Pizza *184*

Mixed Bean Chili *186*

Split Peas with Onions *188*

Polenta Tart with Herb Crust *190*

Mushroom Risotto *192*

Tempeh Noodle Bowl *194*

Tofu Moussaka *196*

Pasta with Tomato & Basil Sauce *198*

Warm Chickpea & Spinach Salad *200*

Roasted Butternut Squash *202*

Eggplant Stew with Polenta *204*

Stir-Fried Rice with Green Vegetables *206*

Spanish Tortilla *208*

Tagliatelle with Hazelnut Pesto *210*

Tofu Stir-Fry *212*

Baked Root Vegetable & Rosemary Cake *214*

Vegetable Main Dishes

Sweet & Sour Noodles

 SERVES 4

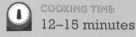 PREP TIME: 10 minutes

COOKING TIME: 12–15 minutes

nutritional information per serving	254 cal, 6g fat, 1.5g sat fat, 13.5g total sugars, 2.3g salt, 3.5g fiber, 40g carbs, 7g protein

These Chinese-style noodles make a wonderful vegetarian dinner, with plenty of flavor and vitamin C.

INGREDIENTS

5 ounces dried medium egg noodles

2 teaspoons sunflower oil

1 large red bell pepper, seeded and thinly sliced

1½ cups bean sprouts

5 scallions, thinly sliced

3 tablespoons Chinese rice wine or dry sherry

salt, to taste

sauce

3 tablespoons light soy sauce

2 tablespoons honey

2 tablespoons tomato paste

2 teaspoons cornstarch

2 teaspoons sesame oil

½ cup vegetable stock

1. Bring a large saucepan of lightly salted water to a boil. Add the noodles, bring back to a boil, and cook according to the package directions, until tender but still firm to the bite. Drain.

2. To make the sauce, put the soy sauce, honey, tomato paste, cornstarch, and sesame oil into a small bowl and mix together until smooth, then stir in the stock.

3. Heat the sunflower oil in a large wok or heavy skillet. Add the red bell pepper and stir-fry for 4 minutes, until soft. Add the bean sprouts and stir-fry for 1 minute. Add the noodles and scallions, then pour the wine and sauce over the vegetables and noodles. Toss together over the heat for 1–2 minutes, until the sauce is simmering and thickened and the noodles are heated all the way through. Serve immediately.

Fuller for longer

Extra low sat fat

Spicy Black-Eyed Peas

 SERVES 4

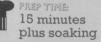 PREP TIME:
15 minutes
plus soaking

COOKING TIME:
2¼–2½ hours

nutritional information per serving	440 cal, 4.5g fat, 0.8g sat fat, 22g total sugars, 2.9g salt, 13g fiber, 72g carbs, 23g protein

Black-eyed peas are one of the most flavorsome legumes, and this fiber-rich recipe makes the most of them.

INGREDIENTS

2 cups black-eyed peas, soaked overnight in cold water

1 tablespoon vegetable oil

2 onions, chopped

1 tablespoon honey

2 tablespoons molasses

¼ cup dark soy sauce

1 teaspoon dry mustard

¼ cup tomato paste

2 cups vegetable stock

1 bay leaf

1 sprig each of rosemary, thyme, and sage

1 small orange

1 tablespoon cornstarch

2 red bell peppers, seeded and diced

pepper, to taste

2 tablespoons chopped fresh flat-leaf parsley, to garnish

1. Preheat the oven to 300°F. Rinse the peas and put in a saucepan. Cover with water, bring to a boil, and boil rapidly for 10 minutes. Drain and put in an ovenproof casserole dish.

2. Meanwhile, heat the oil in a skillet and sauté the onions for 5 minutes. Stir in the honey, molasses, soy sauce, mustard, and tomato paste. Pour in the stock, bring to a boil, and pour it over the beans.

3. Tie together the bay leaf and herbs with a clean piece of string and add to the beans. Using a vegetable peeler, pare off three pieces of orange rind, mix into the beans, and season with pepper. Cover and cook in the preheated oven for 1 hour.

4. Extract the juice from the orange and blend with the cornstarch to form a paste. Stir into the beans along with the red bell peppers. Cover and cook in the oven for 1 hour, or until the sauce is rich and thick and the beans are tender. Discard the herbs and orange rind. Garnish with chopped parsley and serve immediately.

Fuller for longer

Extra low sat fat

Super low calorie

Wheat, gluten
& dairy free

Butternut Squash & Lentil Stew

SERVES 4

PREP TIME:
10 minutes

COOKING TIME:
35 minutes

nutritional information per serving	234 cal, 8g fat, 0.8g sat fat, 9g total sugars, 1.6g salt, 6g fiber, 26.5g carbs, 11g protein

Brown lentils have a meaty flavor, and they are a good source of both iron and protein for vegetarians.

INGREDIENTS

1 tablespoon olive oil
1 onion, diced
3 garlic cloves, finely chopped
2 tablespoons tomato paste
2 teaspoons ground cumin
1 teaspoon ground cinnamon
1 teaspoon salt
¼ teaspoon cayenne pepper
½ butternut squash, diced
½ cup brown lentils
2 cups gluten-free vegetable stock
1 tablespoon lemon juice

to garnish
¼ cup low-fat plain soy yogurt
2 tablespoons finely chopped cilantro
2 tablespoons slivered almonds

1. Heat the oil in a large saucepan over medium–high heat. Add the onion and garlic and cook, stirring occasionally, for about 5 minutes or until soft.

2. Add the tomato paste, cumin, cinnamon, salt, and cayenne and give it a quick stir. Add the squash, lentils, and stock and bring to a boil. Reduce the heat to low and simmer, uncovered, stirring occasionally, for about 25 minutes, until the squash and lentils are tender.

3. Just before serving, stir in the lemon juice. Serve hot, garnished with a dollop of the yogurt and a sprinkling of the cilantro and almonds.

Super low calorie

Spicy Ciabatta Pizza

 SERVES 4

PREP TIME:
15 minutes

COOKING TIME:
35–40 minutes

nutritional information per serving	349 cal, 12g fat, 5g sat fat, 10g total sugars, 1.9g salt, 5g fiber, 41g carbs, 18g protein

Pizza is a family favorite, and this version is a healthy, nutrient-rich take on the classic cheese pizza.

INGREDIENTS

1 (14½-ounce) can diced tomatoes

1 garlic clove, crushed

1 red bell pepper, seeded and chopped

1 green bell pepper, seeded and chopped

½ teaspoon hot smoked paprika

1 ciabatta loaf

8 ounces reduced-fat mozzarella cheese, thinly sliced

2 tablespoons capers, drained, or 12 pitted ripe black olives

1½ tablespoons olive oil

½ teaspoon dried oregano

arugula or basil leaves, to serve

1. Put the tomatoes, garlic, bell peppers, and smoked paprika in a saucepan over medium heat. Bring to a boil, then reduce the heat and simmer for 20–25 minutes, or until thick and most of the liquid has evaporated.

2. Preheat the oven to 425°F. Slice the loaf in half lengthwise and put the two pieces, cut sides up, on a baking sheet. Spread with the tomato sauce, then top with the mozzarella slices and capers or olives.

3. Mix together the olive oil and oregano and drizzle the mixture over the top of the loaves. Bake in the preheated oven for 10–12 minutes, or until crisp and brown around the edges and the cheese is melted and bubbling. Serve immediately, sprinkled with arugula or basil leaves.

Bean Burgers

 SERVES 4

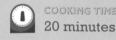 PREP TIME: 15 minutes

COOKING TIME: 20 minutes

nutritional information per serving	111 cal, 4g fat, 0.5g sat fat, 3.5g total sugars, 0.6g salt, 6g fiber, 13g carbs, 5g protein

Satisfy your appetite with these great tasting homemade burgers that will taste far better than those you buy.

INGREDIENTS

1 tablespoon sunflower oil, plus extra for brushing

1 onion, finely chopped

1 garlic clove, finely chopped

1 teaspoon ground coriander

1 teaspoon ground cumin

1⅔ cups finely chopped white mushrooms

1 (15-ounce) can cranberry or red kidney beans, drained and rinsed

2 tablespoons chopped fresh flat-leaf parsley

all-purpose flour, for dusting

salt and pepper, to taste

hamburger buns and salad, to serve

1. Heat the oil in a heavy skillet over medium heat. Add the onion and cook, stirring frequently, for 5 minutes, or until softened. Add the garlic, coriander, and cumin and cook, stirring, for an additional minute. Add the mushrooms and cook, stirring frequently, for 4–5 minutes, until all the liquid has evaporated. Transfer to a bowl.

2. Put the beans in a small bowl and mash with a fork. Stir into the mushroom mixture with the parsley and season with salt and pepper.

3. Preheat the broiler to medium–high. Divide the mixture equally into four portions, dust lightly with flour, and shape into flat, round patties. Brush with oil and cook under the broiler for 4–5 minutes on each side. Serve in hamburger buns with salad.

1

2

3

BE PREPARED

These will freeze well so make a double batch. Open freeze on a tray, then transfer to a rigid container. Freeze for up to three months. Cook from frozen.

Fuller for longer

Extra low sat fat

Super low calorie

Wheat, gluten
& dairy free

Spicy Corn Chowder

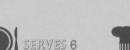 SERVES 6

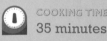 PREP TIME:
15 minutes

COOKING TIME:
35 minutes

nutritional information per serving	156 cal, 8g fat, 1g sat fat, 7g total sugars, 0.7g salt, 4g fiber, 20g carbs, 8g protein

A meal in a bowl, this chowder packs in a huge variety of vegetables that will keep you feeling full for hours.

INGREDIENTS

1 tablespoon olive oil

1 onion, diced

2 garlic cloves, finely chopped

2 carrots, diced

2 celery stalks, diced

1 red bell pepper, seeded and diced

3 cups frozen corn kernels

¾ teaspoon salt

½ teaspoon chili powder

4 cups gluten-free vegetable stock

8 ounces silken tofu, drained

2 tablespoons chopped fresh cilantro, to garnish

3 scallions, thinly sliced, to garnish

1. Heat the oil in a large skillet over medium–high heat. Add the onion and garlic and cook, stirring occasionally, for about 5 minutes, or until soft.

2. Add the carrots, celery, bell pepper, corn, salt, chili powder, and stock. Bring to a boil, reduce the heat to medium–low and simmer, uncovered, for about 20 minutes, or until the vegetables are soft.

3. In a blender or food processor, puree the tofu with a ladleful of the soup. Stir the puree into the soup and simmer for about 5 minutes, or until heated through. Serve hot, garnished with the cilantro and scallions.

1

2

3

BE PREPARED

Buy bell peppers in season, then dice, bag, and freeze them so you'll always have some on hand.

Fuller for longer

Extra low sat fat

Super low calorie

Wheat, gluten
& dairy free

Tofu Steak with Fennel & Orange

 SERVES 4

PREP TIME:
15 minutes

COOKING TIME:
6–8 minutes

nutritional information
per serving

141 cal, 8g fat, 1g sat fat, 6g total sugars, 0.2g salt, 3g fiber,
8g carbs, 10g protein

*Tofu is bland but easily takes on other flavors,
so it is ideal for using with hot spices, such as
Cajun seasoning or Moroccan harissa.*

INGREDIENTS

12 ounces extra firm tofu, drained

1 tablespoon gluten-free harissa paste

2 teaspoons extra virgin olive oil

1 large orange

1 fennel bulb, very thinly sliced

1 small red onion, thinly sliced

8 pitted ripe black olives, halved

chopped fresh mint, to garnish

1. Preheat the broiler to high. Put the tofu on a clean dish towel and press lightly to remove any excess moisture.

2. Cut the tofu into four thick triangles. Mix the harissa with the oil. Brush this mixture over the tofu.

3. Lift the tofu steaks onto a baking sheet and cook under the preheated broiler for 6–8 minutes, turning once, until golden brown.

4. Meanwhile, use a sharp knife to cut all the rind and white pith from the orange and carefully remove the segments from the membranes, catching the juice in a bowl.

5. Put the orange segments, fennel, onion, and olives in bowl. Mix thoroughly to combine and then divide the mixture among four serving plates.

6. Place the tofu steaks on top, drizzle with the reserved orange juice, and garnish with chopped fresh mint to serve.

Stuffed Tomatoes

 SERVES 4

PREP TIME: 15 minutes

COOKING TIME: 15–20 minutes

nutritional information per serving	253 cal, 11g fat, 1g sat fat, 13g total sugars, trace salt, 3g fiber, 37g carbs, 5g protein

These light and tasty rice-filled tomatoes make an ideal summer meal. Half quantities make a great appetizer.

INGREDIENTS

4 beefsteak tomatoes

2 cups cooked rice

8 scallions, chopped

3 tablespoons chopped fresh mint

2 tablespoons chopped fresh flat-leaf parsley

3 tablespoons pine nuts

3 tablespoons raisins

2 teaspoons olive oil

salt and pepper, to taste

1. Cut the tomatoes in half, then scoop out the seeds and discard.

2. Stand the tomatoes, upside down, on paper towels for a few moments so the juices drain out.

3. Preheat the oven to 375°F. Turn the tomatoes the right way up and season the insides with salt and pepper.

4. Mix together the rice, scallions, mint, parsley, pine nuts, and raisins in a bowl. Spoon the mixture into the tomato cups.

5. Drizzle with a little olive oil, then arrange the tomatoes on a baking sheet or baking dish. Cook in the preheated oven for 15–20 minutes, or until they are tender and cooked through.

6. Transfer the tomatoes to serving plates and serve immediately.

1

4

4

HEALTHY HINT

Using brown rice in the stuffing will increase the fiber and vitamin content of your meal.

Super low calorie

Broccoli Pizza

 SERVES 8

 PREP TIME:
20 minutes
plus rising

COOKING TIME:
18 minutes

nutritional information per serving	274 cal, 9g fat, 4g sat fat, 2g total sugars, 1.3g salt, 3g fiber, 40.5g carbs, 11g protein

One secret to healthier pizza is to have vegetables in the topping—and our broccoli version certainly achieves that.

INGREDIENTS

1 cup lukewarm water
1½ teaspoons active dry yeast
2 teaspoons salt
1 teaspoon sugar
1 tablespoon olive oil
3 cups white bread flour, plus extra for dusting
2 sprays olive oil spray

topping
2 cups small broccoli florets
2 teaspoons olive oil
1 red onion, thinly sliced
1 garlic clove, finely chopped
1 tablespoon chopped fresh oregano
1¼ cups shredded Swiss cheese
¼–½ teaspoon crushed red pepper flakes

1. To make the pizza crust, combine the lukewarm water, yeast, salt, and sugar in a large mixing bowl and stir well. Let rest for about 10 minutes, until bubbly. Stir in the olive oil, then gradually mix in the flour with an electric mixer or food processor until the mixture comes together in a ball. Turn the dough out onto a lightly floured surface and knead, adding a little more flour, if needed, for a minute or two, or until firm. Wash and dry the mixing bowl, then spray with olive oil. Put the dough in the bowl, cover with plastic wrap, and let rise in a warm place for about an hour, or until doubled in size.

2. Preheat the oven to 450°F. Spray a baking sheet with olive oil. Roll out the dough into a large rectangle and place it on the prepared baking sheet. Bake in the preheated oven for about 8 minutes, or until just beginning to brown.

3. Meanwhile, put the broccoli in a microwave-safe bowl along with ¼ cup of water and cover tightly with plastic wrap. Microwave on high for about 3 minutes, or until the broccoli is just tender. Drain and chop the broccoli into small pieces.

4. Heat the olive oil in a skillet over medium heat. Add the onion and garlic. Cook, stirring occasionally, for about 5 minutes, or until soft. Remove from the heat and stir in the oregano. Spread the onion mixture evenly onto the partly baked pizza crust and top it with the broccoli, then sprinkle with the cheese and red pepper flakes. Bake for about 10 minutes, or until the cheese is melted, bubbling, and golden brown. Slice and serve immediately.

Fuller for longer

Extra low sat fat

Super low calorie

Mixed Bean Chili

 SERVES 5

 PREP TIME:
10 minutes
plus soaking

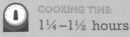 COOKING TIME:
1¼–1½ hours

nutritional information per serving	113 cal, 0.7g fat, 0.1g sat fat, 4.5g total sugars, 0.1g salt, 8g fiber, 18g carbs, 9g protein

An incredibly easy-to-cook bowlful of tasty goodness, ideal for a cold winter evening.

INGREDIENTS

1 cup dried mixed beans, such as red kidney, pinto, cannellini, and chickpeas
1 red onion, diced
1 garlic clove, crushed
1 tablespoon hot chili powder
1 (14½-ounce) can diced tomatoes
1 tablespoon tomato paste
¼ cup low-fat plain yogurt, to garnish
soft flour tortilla wraps, to serve

1. Soak the beans overnight or for 8 hours in a large bowl of cold water. Drain, rinse, and put the beans into a large saucepan. Cover with cold water, then bring to a boil and boil rapidly for 10 minutes. Reduce the heat, cover, and simmer for an additional 45 minutes, or until tender. Drain.

2. Put the cooked beans, onion, garlic, chili powder, tomatoes, and tomato paste into a saucepan and bring to a boil. Reduce the heat, cover, and simmer for 20–25 minutes, or until the onion is tender.

3. Ladle the chili into bowls and top each bowl with some of the yogurt. Serve immediately with soft flour tortilla wraps.

COOK'S NOTE
To save time, use canned beans, drained and rinsed, and skip step 1—two (15-ounce) cans will be equivalent.

Split Peas with Onions

 SERVES 4

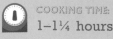 PREP TIME: 10 minutes

COOKING TIME: 1–1¼ hours

nutritional information per serving	252 cals, 7g fat, 1g sat fat, 4g total sugars, 1.3g salt, 6g fiber, 37g carbs, 13g protein

This is a perfect combination of high-protein and high-fiber legumes, healthy oils, and antioxidant-rich spices.

INGREDIENTS

1 cup yellow split peas, washed

½ teaspoon ground turmeric

1 teaspoon ground coriander

1 teaspoon salt

4 curry leaves

2 tablespoons oil

½ teaspoon asafoetida powder (optional)

1 teaspoon cumin seeds

2 onions, chopped

2 garlic cloves, crushed

½ -inch piece fresh ginger, grated

½ teaspoon garam masala

1. Put the split peas in a large saucepan. Pour in enough water to cover by 1 inch.

2. Bring to a boil and use a spoon to remove any of the foam that has formed.

3. Add the turmeric, ground coriander, salt, and curry leaves. Simmer for 1 hour. The split peas should be tender, but not mushy.

4. Heat the oil in heavy skillet. Add the asafoetida, if using, and sauté for 30 seconds. Add the cumin seeds and sauté until they start popping. Add the onions and sauté until golden brown.

5. Add the garlic, ginger, garam masala, and split pea mixture to the pan and cook for 2 minutes. Serve immediately.

COOK'S NOTE
If you can't find asafoetida powder, try using celery salt as a substitute.

Polenta Tart with Herb Crust

Extra low sat fat

Super low calorie

 SERVES 4

PREP TIME:
15 minutes

COOKING TIME:
20–25 minutes

nutritional information per serving	300 cal, 7g fat, 2g sat fat, 5g total sugars, 0.2g salt, 4g fiber, 52g carbs, 7g protein

This polenta tart makes a change from pastry or pizza crust—and it's gluten free, too!

INGREDIENTS

olive oil, for greasing and brushing

3½ cups boiling water

1½ cups instant polenta

1 tablespoon chopped fresh oregano, plus extra to garnish

1 small yellow bell pepper, seeded and thinly sliced

1 small red onion, thinly sliced

1 small zucchini, thinly sliced

2 tomatoes, sliced

4 ounces reduced-fat mozzarella cheese, diced

8 ripe black olives, pitted and halved

salt and pepper, to taste

1. Preheat the oven to 400°F. Grease a large baking sheet. Pour the water into a large saucepan, add a pinch of salt, and bring to a boil over high heat. Add the polenta in a steady stream, stirring continuously until smooth.

2. Reduce the heat and stir continuously for 4–5 minutes, or until the polenta is thick and smooth. Remove from the heat and stir in the oregano. Season with pepper. Spoon the polenta onto the prepared baking sheet and spread out in a 12-inch circle, raising the edges slightly.

3. Arrange the bell pepper, onion, zucchini, and tomatoes over the polenta and add the mozzarella. Top the tart with the olives and brush lightly with olive oil.

4. Bake in the preheated oven for 15–20 minutes, or until bubbling and golden brown. Garnish with oregano and serve immediately.

1

2

3

COOK'S NOTE
Be careful when cooking the polenta because it tends to splash as it boils, so keep the heat low.

Mushroom Risotto

 SERVES 1

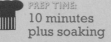 PREP TIME:
10 minutes
plus soaking

COOKING TIME:
40–45 minutes

nutritional information per serving	435 cal, 11.4g fat, 4.5g sat fat, 5g total sugars, 0.7g salt, 7g fiber, 51g carbs, 16g protein

A healthier take on the classic Italian risotto, with much less saturated fat.

INGREDIENTS

1 tablespoon dried porcini

1 teaspoon olive oil

1 teaspoon butter

½ onion, finely chopped

1 small garlic clove, finely chopped

6 ounces mixed fresh mushrooms, such as cremini, shiitake, and button

⅓ cup risotto rice

1 cup vegetable stock

¼ cup dry white wine or extra stock (optional)

1 small zucchini, chopped

1 teaspoon chopped fresh flat-leaf parsley

1 teaspoon freshly grated Parmesan cheese

pepper, to taste

1. Put the dried mushrooms in a bowl, cover with water, and let soak for 30 minutes.

2. About 5 minutes before the soaking time is up, heat the oil and butter in a large, lidded skillet and sauté the onion and garlic over medium heat for about 5 minutes, or until soft. Add the fresh mushrooms and season with pepper, stir well, and cook for 1–2 minutes.

3. Add the rice and soaked mushrooms with their soaking water, stock, and wine, if using, and stir. Cover and simmer for 20 minutes, adding a little extra stock or water if it looks dry. Add the zucchini and continue to simmer for an additional 10 minutes.

4. When the rice is tender and creamy, stir in the parsley and cheese. Serve immediately.

Fuller for longer

Extra low sat fat

Super low calorie

Tempeh Noodle Bowl

 SERVES 4

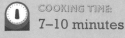 PREP TIME:
10 minutes

COOKING TIME:
7–10 minutes

nutritional information per serving	250 cal, 4g fat, 0.5g sat fat, 3g total sugars, 0.8g salt, 2.5g fiber, 42g carbs, 11g protein

Tempeh has an even higher protein content than tofu and is naturally cholesterol free.

INGREDIENTS

4 ounces shiitake mushrooms

2 tablespoons miso paste

2½ cups boiling water

3 cups diagonally halved snow peas

7 ounces tempeh or smoked tofu, cubed

1 bunch scallions, sliced

6 ounces dried udon or soba noodles

salt, to taste

1. Remove the stems from the mushrooms and cut a deep cross in the top of the caps.

2. Put the miso and water in a large saucepan and stir thoroughly to dissolve the miso. Put the pan over high heat and bring back to a boil. Add the mushrooms and snow peas and cook for 2–3 minutes to soften. Stir the tempeh and scallions into the pan and cook for another 2 minutes.

3. Meanwhile, cook the noodles in a saucepan of lightly salted boiling water for 3–4 minutes, or cook according to the package directions, until tender. Drain well, then divide among four warm serving bowls.

4. Spoon the tempeh-and-vegetable mixture over the noodles and serve immediately.

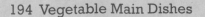

COOK'S NOTE

If you can buy fresh udon or soba noodles, these take only one to two minutes to cook.

Tofu Moussaka

Fuller for longer

Extra low sat fat

Super low calorie

 SERVES 4

PREP TIME:
20 minutes

COOKING TIME:
1½–2 hours

nutritional information per serving	273 cal, 9.5g fat, 2.7g sat fat, 16g total sugars, 0.3g salt, 4.5g fiber, 31g carbs, 16g protein

Who doesn't love the delicious indulgence of moussaka? And the good news is that this is also a low-fat treat.

INGREDIENTS

3 small russet potatoes, scrubbed

¼ cup lemon juice

1 teaspoon canola oil or vegetable oil

1 teaspoon sugar

2 teaspoons crushed garlic

1 teaspoon ground cumin

2 tablespoons dried oregano

3 cups diced eggplant

1 cup sliced onion

1 cup seeded and diced mixed bell peppers

¾ cup canned diced tomatoes

1¾ cups plain yogurt

2 tablespoons cornstarch

2 tablespoons dry mustard

7 ounces silken tofu, sliced

1 small beefsteak tomato, thinly sliced

pepper, to taste

1. Preheat the oven to 375°F. Bake the potatoes in their skins in the oven for 45 minutes, then remove and let cool. Cut into thin slices.

2. Mix together the lemon juice, oil, sugar, garlic, cumin, and oregano in a small bowl, then lightly brush over the diced eggplant, reserving the remaining mixture. Spread out on a baking sheet and bake in the preheated oven for 15 minutes. Leave the oven on.

3. Heat the reserved lemon juice mixture in a skillet over high heat, add the onion and bell peppers, and cook, stirring occasionally, until lightly browned. Add the canned tomatoes, reduce the heat, and simmer for 4 minutes.

4. In a separate saucepan, whisk together the yogurt and cornstarch, then bring to a boil, whisking continuously (to prevent the yogurt from separating) until the yogurt boils and thickens. When the yogurt has thickened, remove from the heat and whisk in the dry mustard.

5. In an ovenproof dish, make layers of the potatoes, eggplant, onion-and-bell pepper mixture, and tofu, adding yogurt sauce between each layer. Finish with a layer of tomato slices and top with the remaining yogurt sauce.

6. Bake in the preheated oven for 20–25 minutes, or until golden brown on top. Season with pepper and serve immediately.

Pasta with Tomato & Basil Sauce

 SERVES 4   PREP TIME: 15 minutes   COOKING TIME: 30–35 minutes

nutritional information per serving	351 cal, 5g fat, 0.8g sat fat, 6g total sugars, trace salt, 5g fiber, 70g carbs, 11.5g protein

This tomato sauce is rich in potassium, which will help beat fluid retention and high blood pressure.

INGREDIENTS

2 fresh rosemary sprigs

2 garlic cloves, unpeeled

4 tomatoes, halved

1 tablespoon olive oil

1 tablespoon sun-dried tomato paste

12 fresh basil leaves, plus extra to garnish

1½ pounds fresh farfalle (pasta bow ties) or 12 ounces dried farfalle

salt and pepper, to taste

1. Put the rosemary, garlic, and tomatoes, skin side up, in a shallow roasting pan.

2. Preheat the broiler to medium. Drizzle with the oil and cook under the preheated broiler for 20 minutes, or until the tomato skins are slightly charred.

3. Peel the skin from the tomatoes. Coarsely chop the tomato flesh and put in a saucepan. Squeeze the pulp from the garlic cloves and mix with the tomato flesh and sun-dried tomato paste.

4. Coarsely tear the fresh basil leaves into smaller pieces and then stir them into the sauce. Season with a little salt and pepper.

5. Put a saucepan of lightly salted water over high heat and bring to a boil. Add the farfalle, bring back to a boil, and cook for 10 minutes, or until tender but still firm to the bite.

6. Gently heat the tomato and basil sauce. Transfer the farfalle to serving plates and garnish with the basil. Serve with the tomato sauce over the top.

Fuller for longer

Super low calorie

Warm Chickpea & Spinach Salad

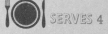 SERVES 4

PREP TIME:
15 minutes

COOKING TIME:
10 minutes

nutritional information per serving	301 cal, 16.7g fat, 5.5g sat fat, 3.1g total sugars, 2.1g salt, 5.9g fiber, 17.4g carbs, 24g protein

A colorful salad that is rich in protein and fiber, with a full, spicy flavor.

INGREDIENTS

1 tablespoon olive oil

1 garlic clove, finely chopped

½ teaspoon crushed red pepper flakes

1 cup halved baby plum tomatoes

2 cups diced reduced-fat halloumi or Muenster cheese

1 slice whole-wheat bread, cut into ½-inch squares

1 tablespoon sesame seeds

2½ cups baby spinach leaves

1 small red onion, thinly sliced

1 (15-ounce) can chickpeas, drained and rinsed

1. Preheat the oven to 400°F. Mix 2 teaspoons of the olive oil with the garlic, red pepper flakes, tomatoes, and cheese in a bowl, stirring to coat evenly. Spread the tomatoes and cheese over one half of a baking sheet.

2. Put the bread cubes with the remaining oil and sesame seeds in a bowl and stir to coat. Spread the bread cubes on the other half of the sheet.

3. Bake in the preheated oven for about 10 minutes, or until the tomatoes are tender, the cheese is starting to brown, and the bread cubes are crisp.

4. Meanwhile, arrange the spinach leaves in a wide serving dish, or individual dishes, and spoon the onion and chickpeas on top.

5. Remove the baking sheet from the oven and spoon the tomatoes, cheese, and bread cubes over the salad. Serve immediately.

1

2

4

**SOMETHING
DIFFERENT**
Replace the
chickpeas with
canned red
kidney beans
and omit the
cheese.

Extra low sat fat

Super low calorie

Roasted Butternut Squash

 SERVES 4

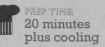 PREP TIME:
20 minutes
plus cooling

COOKING TIME:
1¼ hours

nutritional information per serving	97 cal, 0.8g fat, 0.3g sat fat, 11g total sugars, 0.4g salt, 6g fiber, 18g carbs, 5g protein

Squash, stuffed with high-fiber beans and vegetables, is an ideal slimmer's dinner, both filling and satisfying.

INGREDIENTS

1 small butternut squash

1 onion, chopped

2–3 garlic cloves, crushed

4 small tomatoes, chopped

1 cup chopped cremini mushrooms

½ cup drained, rinsed, and coarsely chopped canned lima beans

1 zucchini, trimmed and shredded

1 tablespoon chopped fresh oregano, plus extra to garnish

2 tablespoons tomato paste

1¼ cups water

4 scallions, chopped

1 tablespoon Worcestershire or hot pepper sauce, or to taste

pepper, to taste

1. Preheat the oven to 375°F. Prick the squash all over with the tip of a sharp knife, then roast for 40 minutes, or until tender. Remove from the oven and let rest until cool enough to handle.

2. Cut the squash in half, scoop out and discard the seeds, then scoop out some of the flesh, making hollows in both halves. Chop the cooked flesh and put in a bowl. Place the two halves side by side in a large roasting pan.

3. Add the onion, garlic, chopped tomatoes, and mushrooms to the cooked squash. Add the coarsely chopped lima beans, shredded zucchini, chopped oregano, season with pepper, and mix well. Spoon the filling into the two halves of the squash, packing it down as firmly as possible.

4. Mix the tomato paste with the water, scallions, and Worcestershire sauce in a small bowl and pour around the squash.

5. Cover loosely with a large sheet of aluminum foil and bake for 30 minutes, or until piping hot. Serve, divided equally among four warm plates, garnished with extra chopped oregano.

Fuller for longer

Extra low sat fat

Eggplant Stew with Polenta

 SERVES 4

PREP TIME:
10 minutes

COOKING TIME:
1 hour

nutritional information per serving	440 cal, 12g fat, 1.5g sat fat, 16g total sugars, 0.2g salt, 8g fiber, 65g carbs, 12g protein

This tasty Mediterranean stew has so much flavor, meat eaters won't notice the lack of meat.

INGREDIENTS

1 eggplant, diced
3 tablespoons olive oil
1 large onion, thinly sliced
1 carrot, diced
2 garlic cloves, chopped
2 cups sliced mushrooms
2 teaspoons ground coriander
2 teaspoons cumin seeds
1 teaspoon chili powder
1 teaspoon ground turmeric
2½ cups canned diced tomatoes
1¼ cups vegetable stock
½ cup chopped dried apricots
1 (15-ounce) can chickpeas, drained and rinsed
2 tablespoons cilantro, to garnish

polenta
5 cups hot vegetable stock
1¼ cups instant polenta

1. Preheat the broiler to medium. Toss the eggplant in 1 tablespoon of the oil and arrange in the broiler pan. Cook under the preheated broiler for 20 minutes, turning occasionally, until softened and beginning to blacken around the edges—brush with more oil if the eggplant becomes too dry.

2. Heat the remaining oil in a large, heavy saucepan over medium heat. Add the onion and sauté, stirring occasionally, for 8 minutes, or until soft and golden. Add the carrot, garlic, and mushrooms and cook for 5 minutes. Add the spices and cook, stirring continously, for an additional minute.

3. Add the tomatoes and stock, stir well, and bring to a boil. Reduce the heat and simmer for 10 minutes, or until the sauce begins to thicken and reduce.

4. Add the eggplant, apricots, and chickpeas, partly cover, and cook for an additional 10 minutes, stirring occasionally.

5. Meanwhile, to make the polenta, pour the hot stock into a large saucepan and bring to a boil. Pour in the polenta in a steady stream, stirring continuously with a wooden spoon. Reduce the heat to low and cook for 1–2 minutes, or until the polenta thickens to a mashed potato-like consistency. Serve the stew with the polenta, sprinkled with the fresh cilantro.

Fuller for longer

Super low calorie

Spanish Tortilla

 SERVES 4

PREP TIME:
10 minutes

COOKING TIME:
35–40 minutes

nutritional information per serving	258 cal, 16g fat, 4g sat fat, 2g total sugars, 0.4g salt, 2g fiber, 17g carbs, 13g protein

Eggs, onions, and potatoes have never tasted so delicious, and yet our low-cost omelet is easy to make.

INGREDIENTS

3 red-skinned or white round potatoes, cut into bite-size cubes

1 tablespoon olive oil

1 tablespoon low-fat spread

1 onion, thinly sliced

6 eggs, lightly beaten

salt and pepper, to taste

sliced tomatoes, to serve

1. Cook the potatoes in a saucepan of salted boiling water for 10–12 minutes, or until tender. Drain well and set aside.

2. Meanwhile, heat the oil and spread in a medium skillet with a heatproof handle over medium heat. Add the onion and sauté, stirring occasionally, for 8 minutes, or until soft and golden. Add the potatoes and cook for an additional 5 minutes, stirring to prevent them from sticking. Spread the onions and potatoes evenly over the bottom of the skillet.

3. Preheat the broiler to medium. Season the eggs with salt and pepper and pour them over the onion and potatoes. Cook over medium heat for 5–6 minutes, or until the eggs are just set and the bottom of the tortilla is lightly golden.

4. Place the skillet under the preheated broiler (if the handle is not heatproof, wrap with a double layer of aluminum foil) and cook the top of the tortilla for 2–3 minutes, until it is just set and risen. Cut into wedges and serve with sliced tomatoes.

1

2

3

HEALTHY HINT

Think about buying organic eggs, which contain higher levels of healthy omega-3 fats.

Fuller for longer

Extra low sat fat

Tagliatelle with Hazelnut Pesto

SERVES 4

PREP TIME:
5 minutes

COOKING TIME:
10–12 minutes

nutritional information per serving	522 cal, 22g fat, 2.5g sat fat, 3g total sugars, 0.1g salt, 9g fiber, 71g carbs, 15g protein

Fresh and light, this protein-packed vegetarian main dish is made in a matter of minutes.

INGREDIENTS

pesto
1 garlic clove, coarsely chopped
½ cup hazelnuts
3½ cups wild arugula
¼ cup olive oil
salt and pepper, to taste

12 ounces dried tagliatelle
1 cup fresh or frozen fava beans

1. To make the pesto, put the garlic, hazelnuts, arugula, and oil in a food processor and process to a rough paste. Season with salt and pepper.

2. Bring a large saucepan of lightly salted water to a boil. Add the pasta, return to a boil, and cook for 8–10 minutes, or until tender but still firm to the bite. Add the beans 3–4 minutes before the end of the cooking time.

3. Drain the pasta and beans well, then transfer back to the pan. Add the pesto and toss to coat evenly. Serve immediately.

GOES WELL WITH

If you can find a vegetarian Parmesan-style cheese, grate a few shavings of this over the pasta to add extra flavor.

Low on carbs

Extra low sat fat

Super low calorie

Tofu Stir-Fry

 SERVES 4

PREP TIME:
10 minutes plus
marinating

COOKING TIME:
10–12 minutes

nutritional information per serving	120 cal, 6g fat, 1g sat fat, 5g total sugars, 1.4g salt, 2g fiber, 6g carbs, 9g protein

This vegetable-packed stir-fry is great for anyone on a low-carb diet.

INGREDIENTS

8 ounces firm tofu, cut into bite-size pieces

1 tablespoon sunflower oil

2 scallions, coarsely chopped

1 garlic clove, finely chopped

8 baby corn, halved

2 cups snow peas

4 ounces shiitake mushrooms, thinly sliced

2 tablespoons finely chopped fresh cilantro leaves, to garnish

marinade

2 tablespoons dark soy sauce

1 tablespoon Chinese rice wine

2 teaspoons packed brown sugar

½ teaspoon Chinese five-spice powder

1 fresh red chile, seeded and finely chopped

2 scallions, finely chopped

1 tablespoon grated fresh ginger

1. Put all the marinade ingredients in a large, shallow, nonmetallic dish and stir to mix. Add the bite-size chunks of tofu and turn them over carefully to coat thoroughly in the marinade. Cover the dish with plastic wrap and let rest the tofu in the refrigerator to marinate for 2 hours, turning the chunks over occasionally.

2. Drain the tofu and reserve the marinade. Heat the sunflower oil in a preheated wok or large skillet. Add the tofu and stir-fry over medium–high heat for 2–3 minutes, or until golden. Using a slotted spoon, remove the tofu from the wok and reserve. Add the scallions and garlic and stir-fry for 2 minutes, then add the baby corn and stir-fry for 1 minute. Add the snow peas and mushrooms and stir-fry for an additional 2 minutes.

3. Return the tofu to the wok and add the marinade. Cook gently for 1–2 minutes, or until heated through. Garnish with the chopped fresh cilantro and serve immediately.

Extra low sat fat

Super low calorie

Wheat, gluten
& dairy free

Baked Root Vegetable
& Rosemary Cake

SERVES 4

PREP TIME:
15–20 minutes

COOKING TIME:
1 hour

nutritional information
per serving

104 cal, 2g fat, 0.3g sat fat, 12g total sugars, 0.2g salt,
11g fiber, 19g carbs, 3g protein

*An unusual way to serve a selection of vegetables,
subtly flavored with rosemary and lemon.*

INGREDIENTS

olive oil, for greasing
3 parsnips, shredded
5 carrots, shredded
½ celeriac, shredded
1 onion, coarsely grated
2 tablespoons chopped
fresh rosemary
3 tablespoons lemon juice
salt and pepper, to taste
rosemary sprigs, to garnish

1. Preheat the oven to 375°F. Grease an 8-inch springform cake pan and line with parchment paper.

2. Put the parsnip, carrot, and celeriac in separate, small bowls.

3. Mix together the onion, rosemary, and lemon juice in a small bowl. Add one-third of the onion mixture to each vegetable bowl, season with salt and pepper, and stir to mix evenly.

4. Spoon the parsnips into the prepared pan, spreading evenly and pressing down lightly. Top with the carrots, press lightly, then add the celeriac.

5. Top the cake with a piece of lightly oiled aluminum foil and press down to condense the contents. Tuck the foil over the edges of the pan to seal. Place on a baking sheet and bake in the preheated oven for about 1 hour, or until tender.

6. Remove the foil and turn out the cake onto a warm plate. Let cool for 5 minutes, then slice and serve, garnished with rosemary sprigs.

Desserts

Coffee Ice Cream

SERVES 6

PREP TIME:
15 minutes
plus freezing

COOKING TIME:
No cooking

nutritional information per serving	150 cal, 6g fat, 4g sat fat, 18g total sugars, 0.1g salt, 0g fiber, 18g carbs, 4.5g protein

This is a healthier version of ice cream, with much lower levels of saturated fat.

INGREDIENTS

2 ounces semisweet chocolate
1 cup ricotta cheese
⅓ cup low-fat plain yogurt
⅓ cup granulated sugar
¾ cup strong black coffee, cooled and chilled
½ teaspoon ground cinnamon
dash of vanilla extract

1. Grate the chocolate and reserve. Put the ricotta cheese, yogurt, and sugar in a blender or food processor and process until a smooth puree forms. Transfer to a large bowl and beat in the coffee, cinnamon, vanilla extract, and half of the grated chocolate.

2. Spoon the mixture into a freezerproof container and freeze for 1½ hours, or until slushy. Remove from the freezer, turn into a bowl, and beat. Return to the container and freeze for 1½ hours.

3. Repeat this beating and freezing process two times before serving in scoops, decorated with the remaining grated chocolate. Alternatively, leave in the freezer until 15 minutes before serving, then transfer to the refrigerator to soften slightly before scooping.

FREEZING TIP

Homemade ice cream tends to harden over time if stored in the freezer for too long, but this ice cream will keep well for up to three months in a tightly-sealed container.

Pear & Blueberry Strudel

 SERVES 4   PREP TIME:
20 minutes   COOKING TIME:
40 minutes

nutritional information per serving	255 cal, 10g fat, 4g sat fat, 22g total sugars, 0.4g salt, 5g fiber, 32g carbs, 4g protein

Dessert is an ideal occasion to pack fruit into your diet— this strudel provides 1½ portions of your daily fruit.

INGREDIENTS

2 tablespoons butter

3 firm ripe Bosc pears, cored and chopped

¾ cup blueberries

1 tablespoon packed light brown sugar

½ teaspoon ground cinnamon

1 medium slice whole-wheat bread, toasted and torn into pieces

1½ tablespoons canola oil or sunflower oil

4 sheets of phyllo pastry

confectioners' sugar, for sprinkling

low-fat custard or Greek yogurt, to serve

1. Melt 1 tablespoon of the butter in a large skillet. Add the pears and cook over low heat for 5 minutes, or until tender. Transfer to a bowl and let cool. Gently stir in the blueberries, sugar, and ¼ teaspoon of ground cinnamon.

2. Preheat the oven to 350°F. Put the toast and the remaining cinnamon in a food processor and blend to coarse crumbs. Melt the remaining butter with the oil.

3. Lay one sheet of pastry on a clean work surface and brush lightly with the butter mixture (keep the remaining pastry covered with a damp dish towel while you work to prevent it from drying). Sprinkle with one-third of the crumbs. Repeat two times, then cover with the remaining pastry and brush lightly with the butter mixture.

4. Spoon the pear mixture along one long edge and roll up. Press the ends together to seal and transfer to a baking sheet. Brush with the remaining butter mixture and bake in the preheated oven for 40 minutes, or until crisp. Sprinkle with a little confectioners' sugar. Serve warm with custard or yogurt.

Fuller for longer

Vanilla Soufflé Omelets

 SERVES 4   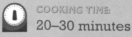 PREP TIME: 10 minutes   COOKING TIME: 20–30 minutes

nutritional information per serving	163 cal, 8g fat, 4.5g sat fat, 8.5g total sugars, 0.5g salt, 2g fiber, 12g carbs, 12g protein

These fluffy, sweet soufflés look substantial, but they are light as air and low in fat and sugar.

INGREDIENTS

8 egg whites

2 tablespoons honey, plus extra for drizzling

1½ teaspoons cornstarch

2 teaspoons vanilla extract

1 cup ricotta cheese

sunflower oil, for brushing

1⅔ cups raspberries

1. Whisk the egg whites in a large, grease-free bowl until they form soft peaks.

2. Add the honey, cornstarch, and vanilla and whisk to mix evenly. Beat the ricotta in a small bowl until smooth, then fold lightly into the egg white mixture.

3. Brush a large, heavy skillet with oil and put over medium heat. Spoon one-quarter of the egg white mixture into the skillet and spread evenly with a spatula.

4. Cook for 3–4 minutes, or until golden underneath. Turn the omelet over and cook for 2–3 minutes on the other side, then sprinkle with one-quarter of the raspberries. Gently lift one side with the spatula and fold the omelet in half to enclose.

5. Cook for an additional few seconds, then flip over onto a serving plate. Keep warm and repeat with the remaining mixture to make four omelets. Serve immediately, drizzled with honey to taste.

1

3

4

SOMETHING DIFFERENT

For a change of flavor, omit the raspberries and add pecans instead, then replace the honey with maple syrup.

Peach Popovers

 SERVES 4   PREP TIME: 15 minutes   COOKING TIME: 15–20 minutes

nutritional information per serving	167 cal, 3g fat, 1g sat fat, 11g total sugars, 0.1g salt, 3g fiber, 31g carbs, 6g protein

A good family dessert that is popular among all ages, and peaches are also a good source of vitamin C.

INGREDIENTS

1 teaspoon sunflower oil, plus extra for greasing

¾ cup all-purpose flour

1 extra-large egg white

1 cup low-fat milk

1 teaspoon vanilla extract

3 peaches, sliced

maple syrup, to serve

1. Preheat the oven to 400°F. Grease 12 cups in a muffin pan.

2. Put the oil, flour, egg white, milk, and vanilla in a large bowl. Beat thoroughly to a smooth, bubbly batter.

3. Put the prepared muffin pan in the preheated oven for 5 minutes. Remove the pan from the oven and quickly divide the peach slices among the cups of the pan and pour the batter evenly into each cup.

4. Bake the popovers for 15–20 minutes, or until well risen, crisp, and golden brown.

5. Remove the popovers carefully from the pan with a small spatula. Serve immediately with maple syrup.

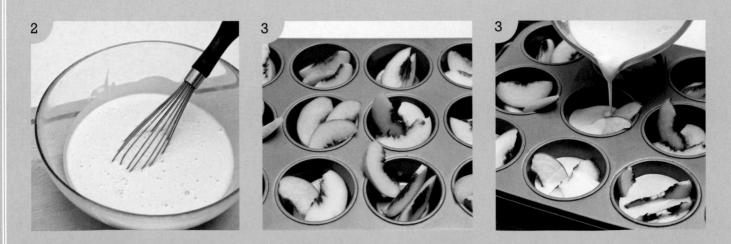

COOK'S NOTE
It's important to thoroughly grease and preheat the pan or the batter may stick. Silicone molds are also a good idea because they are less likely to stick.

Extra low sat fat

Wheat, gluten & dairy free

Red Wine Sorbet

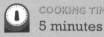 SERVES 6

PREP TIME:
15 minutes
plus freezing

COOKING TIME:
5 minutes

nutritional information per serving	166 cal, 0g fat, 0g sat fat, 22g total sugars, trace salt, trace fiber, 23g carbs, 1g protein

This fruity sorbet makes the perfect finale to a meal, without too many calories, and is completely fat free.

INGREDIENTS

1 orange
1 lemon
2½ cups fruity red wine
⅔ cup firmly packed light brown sugar
1¼ cups water, chilled
2 egg whites, lightly beaten
fresh fruit, to serve

1. Peel the zest from the orange and lemon in strips using a vegetable peeler, being careful not to remove any of the bitter white pith underneath. Put in a saucepan with the red wine and sugar. Heat gently, stirring until the sugar dissolves, then bring to a boil and simmer for 5 minutes. Remove from the heat and stir in the water.

2. Squeeze the juice from the fruit. Stir into the wine mixture. Cover and let sit until completely cool, then strain into a freezerproof container. Cover and freeze for 7–8 hours, or until firm.

3. Working quickly, break the sorbet into chunks and transfer to a food processor. Blend for a few seconds to break down the chunks then, leaving the processor running, gradually pour the egg whites through the feed tube. The mixture will become paler. Continue blending until smooth.

4. Freeze for an additional 3–4 hours, or until firm. Scoop into six chilled glasses or dishes and serve immediately with the fresh fruit.

1

2

3

GOES WELL WITH
This sorbet is great with chilled blueberries—buy from the freezer aisle and defrost until still cold.

Fluffy Lemon Whips

Fuller for longer

Extra low sat fat

Super low calorie

 SERVES 4

PREP TIME:
10 minutes
plus standing

COOKING TIME:
5 minutes

nutritional information per serving	77 cal, 0.8g fat, 0.5g sat fat, 12g total sugars, 0.1g salt, 0g fiber, 13g carbs, 5g protein

Light and fluffy with a refreshing flavor, this simple dessert looks deceptively rich and indulgent.

INGREDIENTS

2 tablespoons lemon juice

3 tablespoons agave syrup or honey

1 mint sprig, plus extra to decorate

2 egg whites

1 teaspoon finely grated lemon rind

⅔ cup low-fat Greek-style yogurt

1. Put the lemon juice, syrup, and mint sprig in a small saucepan over high heat and bring to a boil, stirring. Remove from the heat and let stand for 10 minutes.

2. Meanwhile, put the egg whites in a large, grease-free bowl and whisk with an electric mixer until they hold stiff peaks.

3. Remove the mint from the syrup. Add the lemon rind to the syrup and then gradually drizzle the syrup into the egg whites, beating at high speed.

4. Add the yogurt to the egg white mixture and fold in lightly with a large metal spoon.

5. Spoon the mixture into four tall glasses or individual dishes and top each with a mint sprig. Serve immediately.

1   3   5

COOK'S NOTE
Make sure that no trace of egg yolk gets into the whites, and use a perfectly clean bowl, or the whites will not whisk stiffly.

Wheat, gluten
& dairy free

Coconut Rice Pudding with Pomegranate

 SERVES 4

PREP TIME:
15 minutes
plus chilling

COOKING TIME:
45–50 minutes

nutritional information per serving	154 cal, 6g fat, 4.5g sat fat, 10g total sugars, trace salt, 1.5g fiber, 21g carbs, 2.5g protein

Creamy in texture yet dairy-free, this luxurious dessert is fit for any dinner party.

INGREDIENTS

¼ cup short-grain rice

1 cup canned light coconut milk

1 cup almond milk

2 tablespoons granulated sugar

1 cinnamon stick

2 gelatin sheets

1 pomegranate, separated into seeds

grated nutmeg, to sprinkle

¼ cup pomegranate syrup (optional), to serve

1. Put the rice, coconut milk, almond milk, sugar, and cinnamon in a saucepan over high heat. Bring almost to a boil, stirring, then reduce the heat and cover. Simmer gently, stirring occasionally, for 40–45 minutes, or until most of the liquid is absorbed.

2. Meanwhile, put the gelatin sheets in a bowl and cover with cold water. Let soak for 10 minutes to soften. Drain the sheets, squeezing out any excess moisture, then add to the hot rice mixture and stir lightly until completely dissolved.

3. Spoon the rice mixture into four $^2/_3$-cup metal molds, spreading evenly. Let cool, then cover and chill in the refrigerator until firm.

4. Run a small knife around the edge of each mold. Dip the bottoms briefly into a bowl of hot water, then turn out the rice onto four serving plates.

5. Sprinkle the pomegranate seeds over the rice, then sprinkle with grated nutmeg. Drizzle with a little pomegranate syrup, if using, and serve immediately.

1

2

3

Fuller for longer

Extra low sat fat

Super low calorie

Stuffed Nectarines

 SERVES 4

PREP TIME:
10 minutes

COOKING TIME:
10 minutes

nutritional information per serving	93 cal, 0.2g fat, 0g sat fat, 20g total sugars, 0.1g salt, 4.5g fiber, 16g carbs, 4g protein

A delicious dessert that is low in calories and fat and rich in vitamin C, fiber, and beneficial plant compounds.

INGREDIENTS

4 ripe but firm nectarines or peaches
1¼ cups blueberries
1 cup raspberries
⅔ cup freshly squeezed orange juice
1–2 teaspoons honey, or to taste
1 tablespoon brandy (optional)
¼ cup fat-free Greek yogurt
1 tablespoon finely grated orange rind

1. Preheat the oven to 350°F. Cut the nectarines in half, remove the pits, then put in a shallow ovenproof dish.

2. Mix together the blueberries and raspberries in a bowl and use to fill the hollows left by the removal of the nectarine pits. Spoon any extra berries around the edge.

3. Mix together the orange juice, honey, and brandy, if using, in a small bowl and pour the liquid over the fruit. Blend the yogurt with the grated orange rind in another bowl and let chill in the refrigerator until required.

4. Bake the berry-filled nectarines in the preheated oven for 10 minutes, or until the fruit is hot. Serve immediately with the orange-flavored yogurt.

1   2   3

COOK'S NOTE
It's safer to use a small serrated knife with a blunt end for halving nectarines. Avoid underripe fruit, because it will be hard to remove the pit.

Extra low sat fat

Super low calorie

Wheat, gluten
& dairy free

Golden Polenta Cake

SERVES 12

PREP TIME:
10 minutes
plus cooling

COOKING TIME:
25–30 minutes

nutritional information
per serving

125 cal, 4g fat, 0.7g sat fat, 10g total sugars, 0.19g salt,
0.7g fiber, 20g carbs, 3g protein

Polenta and carrots give this low-fat cake a distinctive texture and rich golden color.

INGREDIENTS

2 tablespoons sunflower oil, plus
extra for greasing

½ cup firmly packed
light brown sugar

finely grated rind of
1 large orange

3 eggs, beaten

3 large carrots, shredded

⅔ cup instant polenta

⅓ cup gluten-free flour blend

1 teaspoon gluten-free
baking powder

syrup
2 tablespoons orange juice

1 tablespoon honey

1. Preheat the oven to 350°F. Grease an 8-inch round deep cake pan and line with parchment paper.

2. Whisk together the oil, sugar, orange rind, and eggs in a large bowl, until smooth and bubbly. Stir in the carrots. Sift in the polenta, flour, and baking powder and fold in evenly.

3. Spoon the batter into the prepared pan. Bake in the preheated oven for 25–30 minutes, or until just firm to the touch and golden brown. Let cool in the pan for 15 minutes.

4. For the syrup, put the orange juice and honey in a small saucepan over low heat. Heat gently until the honey dissolves, without boiling.

5. Transfer the cake to a wire rack, then spoon the syrup evenly over the surface. Let cool completely before serving.

2

3

5

GOES WELL WITH
This cake is great when served with low-fat plain yogurt or low-fat crème fraîche.

Extra low sat fat

Super low calorie

Wheat, gluten
& dairy free

Fresh Fruit Salad with Mini Meringues

 SERVES 4

PREP TIME:
15 minutes
plus cooling

COOKING TIME:
1¼ hours

nutritional information per serving	98 cal, 0.3g fat, 0.1g sat fat, 18g total sugars, 0.1g salt, 4.5g fiber, 18g carbs, 2.5g protein

A virtually fat-free fruit-filled dessert, rich in vitamin C with light and airy, low-calorie meringues.

INGREDIENTS

meringues
1 egg white
⅓ cup superfine sugar

fruit salad
2 cups fresh raspberries
2 teaspoons honey
1 cup water
3 cups mixed fresh fruits, such as raspberries, strawberries, blueberries, and pitted cherries
fresh mint sprigs, to garnish

1. Preheat the oven to 250°F and line a baking sheet with parchment paper.

2. To make the meringues, whisk the egg white in a large, grease-free bowl until stiff, then gradually add the sugar, a spoonful at a time, whisking well after each addition. When all the sugar has been added and the mixture is stiff, spoon into a pastry bag fitted with a large star tip and pipe small whirls onto the lined baking sheet. Alternatively, shape into mounds with 2 teaspoons.

3. Bake in the preheated oven for 1 hour, or until crisp. Let cool before removing from the baking sheet. Store in an airtight container until required.

4. To make the fruit salad, put the raspberries in a saucepan with the honey and water. Bring to a boil, then reduce the heat to a simmer and cook for 5–8 minutes, or until the raspberries have collapsed. Let cool for 5 minutes. Transfer to a food processor and process to form a puree.

5. Press the puree through a fine strainer, adding a little extra water if the puree is too thick.

6. Prepare the fresh fruits and stir into the fruit puree. Stir until lightly coated and serve as four portions with the meringues, decorated with a mint sprig.

Fuller for longer

Extra low sat fat

Granola Fruit Desserts

 SERVES 4

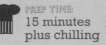 PREP TIME:
15 minutes
plus chilling

COOKING TIME:
10–15 minutes

nutritional information per serving	422 cal, 6g fat, 1g sat fat, 70g total sugars, 0.3g salt, 12g fiber, 80g carbs, 10g protein

Dried fruits are a rich source of fiber, and here they're layered with healthy oats and calcium-rich yogurt.

INGREDIENTS

1 cup dried apricots
⅔ cup dried prunes
1 cup dried peaches
⅔ cup dried apples
3 tablespoons dried cherries
2 cups unsweetened apple juice
6 cardamom pods
6 cloves
1 cinnamon stick, broken
1¼ cups low-fat plain yogurt
1 cup granola
fresh fruit, to decorate

1. To make the fruit compote, put the dried apricots, prunes, peaches, apples, and cherries in a saucepan and pour in the apple juice.

2. Add the cardamom pods, cloves, and cinnamon stick to the pan, bring to a boil, and simmer for 10–15 minutes, or until the fruits are plump and tender.

3. Let the mixture cool completely in the pan, then transfer the mixture to a bowl and let chill in the refrigerator for 1 hour. Remove and discard the spices from the fruits.

4. Spoon the compote into four dessert glasses, layering it alternately with yogurt and granola, finishing with the granola on top.

5. Decorate with fresh fruit and serve immediately.

Extra low sat fat

Wheat, gluten
& dairy free

Fig & Watermelon Salad

 SERVES 4

 PREP TIME:
10 minutes
plus chilling

COOKING TIME:
10 minutes

nutritional information per serving	196 cal, 1g fat, 0.5g sat fat, 44g total sugars, trace salt, 1.5g fiber, 43g carbs, 3g protein

Fresh fruits create a stunning, simple dessert that's high in potassium, vitamin C, and beneficial plant compounds.

INGREDIENTS

⅓ watermelon (about 3¼ pounds)
¾ cup seedless black grapes
4 figs

syrup dressing
1 lime
grated rind and juice of 1 orange
1 tablespoon maple syrup
2 tablespoons honey

1. Cut the watermelon into wedges and scoop out and discard the seeds. Cut the flesh away from the rind, then chop the flesh into 1-inch cubes. Put the watermelon cubes in a bowl with the grapes. Cut each fig lengthwise into eight wedges and add to the bowl.

2. Grate the lime and mix the rind with the orange rind and juice, maple syrup, and honey in a small saucepan. Bring to a boil over low heat. Pour the mixture over the fruit and stir. Let cool. Stir again, cover, and chill in the refrigerator for at least 1 hour, stirring occasionally.

3. Divide the fruit salad equally among four bowls and serve.

1   1   2

SOMETHING DIFFERENT

Instead of grapes, try adding the same amount of fresh blackberries or blueberries for a change.

Fuller for longer

Extra low sat fat

Stuffed Baked Apples

 SERVES 4

PREP TIME:
15 minutes

COOKING TIME:
40 minutes

nutritional information per serving	241 cal, 5g fat, 0.5g sat fat, 35g total sugars, trace salt, 7g fiber, 43g carbs, 4.5g protein

There's nothing more comforting than a baked apple, and stuffed with plump apricots, ginger, and honey, this recipe is a healthy taste sensation.

INGREDIENTS

3 tablespoons blanched almonds

⅓ cup dried apricots

1 piece preserved ginger, drained

1 tablespoon honey

1 tablespoon syrup from the preserved ginger jar

¼ cup rolled oats

4 large Granny Smith apples

1. Preheat the oven to 350°F. Using a sharp knife, chop the almonds, apricots, and preserved ginger finely. Set aside until needed.

2. Put the honey and syrup in a saucepan and heat until the honey has melted. Stir in the oats and cook gently over low heat for 2 minutes. Remove the saucepan from the heat and stir in the almonds, apricots, and preserved ginger.

3. Core the apples, widen the tops slightly, and score horizontally around the circumference of each to prevent the skins from bursting during cooking. Put the apples in a baking dish and fill the cavities with the stuffing. Pour just enough water into the dish to come about one-third of the way up the apples. Bake in the preheated oven for 40 minutes, or until tender. Serve immediately.

1

2

3

SOMETHING DIFFERENT

For a change, use dried cranberries or mixed fruit instead of the apricots.

Fuller for longer

Extra low sat fat

Blueberry & Honey Yogurt

 SERVES 4

PREP TIME:
15 minutes

COOKING TIME:
5 minutes

nutritional information per serving	215 cal, 11g fat, 2g sat fat, 16g total sugars, trace salt, 0.8g fiber, 18g carbs, 9g protein

If you're short of time but still want a tasty dessert, here's a simple and healthy idea that tastes delightful.

INGREDIENTS

3 tablespoons honey
1 cup mixed unsalted nuts
½ cup low-fat Greek-style yogurt
1½ cups fresh blueberries

1. Heat the honey in a small saucepan over medium heat. Add the nuts and stir until they are well coated. Remove from the heat and let cool slightly.

2. Divide the yogurt among four serving bowls, then spoon the nut mixture over the yogurt, top with the blueberries, and serve immediately.

1   1   2

HEALTHY HINT
You could choose plain yogurt with live cultures instead of the Greek yogurt— the bacteria can help resolve some digestive troubles.

Fuller for longer

Apple-Berry Crisp

 SERVES 8

PREP TIME:
10 minutes

COOKING TIME:
45 minutes

nutritional information per serving	237 cal, 7g fat, 4g sat fat, 38g total sugars, 0.4g salt, 4g fiber, 48g carbs, 2g protein

An easy-to-make dessert that is packed with nutrients, our crisp makes a great cold weather treat.

INGREDIENTS

1 spray vegetable oil spray

6 Pippin or other crisp apples, peeled, cored, and sliced

½ cup dried cranberries or dried cherries

¼ cup sugar

½ teaspoon vanilla extract

topping

½ cup all-purpose flour

½ cup firmly packed light brown sugar

½ teaspoon ground cinnamon

pinch of salt

4 tablespoons butter, at room temperature

⅔ cup rolled oats

1. Preheat the oven to 375°F. Spray a baking dish with vegetable oil spray.

2. To make the filling, put the apples, dried fruit, sugar, and vanilla extract into a medium bowl and toss to mix thoroughly. Spread the mixture in the prepared baking dish, overlapping the apples a little as necessary.

3. To make the topping, combine the flour, brown sugar, cinnamon, and salt in the bowl of a food processor or in a large mixing bowl. In the processor, or using two knives, cut the butter into the flour mixture until it resembles coarse bread crumbs. Stir in the oats.

4. Sprinkle the topping evenly over the filling and bake in the preheated oven for about 45 minutes, or until the topping is crisp and beginning to color. Serve immediately.

2

3

4

Extra low sat fat

Super low calorie

Pineapple Carpaccio with Mango Sauce

 SERVES 4

PREP TIME:
10 minutes

COOKING TIME:
No cooking

nutritional information per serving	107 cal, 0.5g fat, 0.1g sat fat, 24g total sugars, trace salt, 4g fiber, 25g carbs, 2.5g protein

Here's a summery, fresh dessert that is easy to prepare. Slice the pineapple as thinly as possible.

INGREDIENTS

1 small pineapple
1 ripe mango
juice of ½ lime
½ cup fat-free plain yogurt

1. Trim the top and bottom from the pineapple, then cut off all the skin and remove the "eyes." Use a large sharp knife to slice the pineapple into thin slices. Arrange the slices overlapping on a wide platter.

2. Peel, pit, and chop the mango flesh, then sprinkle with lime juice and use a blender or food processor to process to a smooth puree.

3. Put the mango puree in a small bowl. Spoon in the yogurt and swirl to create a marbled effect.

4. Put the bowl of mango sauce in the center of the platter. Serve the pineapple with the sauce spooned over the top.

1
2
3

BE PREPARED
This dessert can be
prepared several hours
in advance. Cover the
sliced pineapple and
sauce with plastic wrap
and refrigerate.

Frozen Yogurt Cups

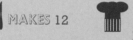 MAKES 12

 PREP TIME:
10 minutes
plus freezing

COOKING TIME:
No cooking

nutritional information per cup	26 cal, 0.4g fat, 0.2g sat fat, 4g total sugars, trace salt, 0.5g fiber, 4g carbs, 2g protein

Packed with calcium and heart-protecting berries, these low-calorie desserts are a real tasty treat.

INGREDIENTS

2 cups low-fat plain yogurt

1½ tablespoons finely grated orange rind

2 cups mixed berries, such as blueberries, raspberries, and strawberries, plus extra to decorate

fresh mint sprigs, to decorate (optional)

1. Set the freezer to its coldest setting at least 2 hours before freezing this dish. Line a 12-cup muffin pan with 12 muffin cups or use small ramekin dishes placed on a baking sheet.

2. Mix together the yogurt and orange rind in a large bowl. Cut any large strawberries into pieces so that they are the same size as the blueberries and raspberries.

3. Add the fruit to the yogurt, then spoon into the cups or ramekins. Freeze for 2 hours, or until just frozen. Decorate with extra fruit and mint sprigs, if using, and serve. Remember to return the freezer to its original setting afterward.

SOMETHING
DIFFERENT
You can use lemon rind
instead of the orange,
if you prefer, or a
mixture of both.

Broiled Fruit Kabobs

 SERVES 4

PREP TIME:
10 minutes
plus marinating

COOKING TIME:
10 minutes

nutritional information per serving	164 cal, 8g fat, 0.5g sat fat, 22g total sugars, trace salt, 3g fiber, 22g carbs, 1g protein

Apart from small berries, most fruits can be broiled this way. Choose firm fruit so they stay in place.

INGREDIENTS

2 tablespoons hazelnut oil

2 tablespoons honey

juice and finely grated rind of 1 lime

2 pineapple slices, cut into chunks

8 strawberries

1 pear, cored and thickly sliced

1 banana, peeled and thickly sliced

2 kiwis, peeled and quartered

1. Preheat the broiler to medium. Mix together the oil, honey, and lime juice and rind in a large, shallow, nonmetallic dish. Add the fruit and turn to coat. Cover and let marinate for 10 minutes.

2. Thread the fruit alternately onto four long metal skewers, beginning with a piece of pineapple and ending with a strawberry.

3. Brush the kabobs with the marinade and cook under the preheated broiler, brushing frequently with the marinade, for 5 minutes. Turn the kabobs over, brush with the remaining marinade, and broil for an additional 5 minutes. Serve immediately.

COOK'S NOTE

Honey varies widely in flavor and the best quality, with a distinctive taste, is usually made from a single type of blossom.

Pistachio Angel Cake

Extra low sat fat

Wheat, gluten
& dairy free

 SERVES 8   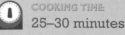 PREP TIME:
20 minutes   COOKING TIME:
25–30 minutes

nutritional information per serving	170 cal, 3g fat, 0.3g sat fat, 22g total sugars, 0.1g salt, 0.3g fiber, 32g carbs, 4g protein

This light, gluten-free cake is great when paired with fresh fruit.

INGREDIENTS

sunflower oil, for greasing
6 egg whites
¾ teaspoon cream of tartar
¾ cup granulated sugar
1 teaspoon vanilla extract
⅓ cup finely chopped pistachio nuts
½ cup rice flour, plus extra for dusting
fresh fruit, to serve

1. Preheat the oven to 325°F. Grease a 1½-quart tube pan and dust lightly with a little flour, tipping out the excess.

2. Whisk the egg whites with an electric mixer in a large, grease-free bowl until they hold soft peaks. Stir the cream of tartar into the sugar in a small bowl, then gradually whisk into the egg whites, beating at high speed until the mixture holds stiff peaks. Beat in the vanilla.

3. In a separate small bowl, stir the pistachios into the flour. Fold the pistachio mixture into the egg white mixture lightly and evenly, using a large metal spoon.

4. Spoon the batter into the prepared pan and tap the pan to remove any large air bubbles. Bake in the preheated oven for 25–30 minutes, or until golden brown and firm to the touch.

5. Turn out the cake onto a wire rack and let cool, upside down, in the pan. When cool, run the tip of a knife around the edges of the cake to loosen, then turn out onto a plate and serve with fresh fruit.

Broiled Cinnamon Oranges

 SERVES 4

 PREP TIME:
5 minutes

 COOKING TIME:
3–5 minutes

nutritional information per serving	88 cal, 0.2g fat, 0g sat fat, 20g total sugars, trace salt, 3.5g fiber, 20g carbs, 1.5g protein

Halved oranges, topped with cinnamon and sugar, will smell absolutely delicious as they broil and are a simple, healthy way to end a meal. They would be equally suited for a breakfast menu, too.

INGREDIENTS

4 large oranges
1 teaspoon ground cinnamon
1 tablespoon raw brown sugar

1. Preheat the broiler to high. Cut the oranges in half and discard any seeds. Using a sharp knife, carefully cut the flesh away from the skin by cutting around the edge of the fruit. Cut across the segments to loosen the flesh into bite-size pieces that will then spoon out easily.

2. Arrange the orange halves, cut side up, in a shallow, flameproof dish. Mix the cinnamon with the sugar in a small bowl and sprinkle evenly over the orange halves.

3. Cook under the preheated broiler for 3–5 minutes, until the sugar has caramelized and is golden and bubbling. Serve immediately.

GOES WELL WITH
Top with a low-fat plain yogurt, mixed with honey, for a special treat.

Banana Split Sundae

 SERVES 2

PREP TIME:
15 minutes
plus freezing

COOKING TIME:
5 minutes

nutritional information per serving	296 cal, 10g fat, 4.5g sat fat, 45g total sugars, 0.3g salt, 6g fiber, 49g carbs, 9g protein

Sundaes need not be off limits—made using high-fiber banana, this is much lower in fat than you'd expect.

INGREDIENTS

2 small bananas
2 teaspoons slivered almonds, toasted

chocolate sauce
2 tablespoons light brown sugar
3 tablespoons unsweetened cocoa powder
⅓ cup low-fat milk
1 ounce semisweet chocolate, chopped
½ teaspoon vanilla extract

1. Peel and dice the bananas, then freeze the diced bananas for 2 hours. Process the frozen bananas in a blender or food processor until creamy. Return the banana puree to the freezer and chill for about 1 hour, or until firm.

2. To make the chocolate sauce, put the sugar, cocoa powder, and milk in a small saucepan and heat to a simmer over medium heat. Reduce the heat to low and cook, stirring continuously, for about 1 minute, or until the sugar and cocoa powder are dissolved. Remove from the heat and stir in the chopped chocolate until it melts. Stir in the vanilla extract. Let the sauce cool slightly.

3. Scoop the banana puree into two bowls, drizzle warm chocolate sauce over the top, and sprinkle with the almonds.

SOMETHING
DIFFERENT
Instead of
almonds, use
chopped mixed
nuts, or crushed
walnuts for a
stronger taste.

Fuller for longer

Oaty Plum Crisp

🍽 SERVES 4

👨‍🍳 PREP TIME:
15 minutes

⏲ COOKING TIME:
20–25 minutes

nutritional information per serving	306 cal, 8g fat, 4g sat fat, 23g total sugars, 0.2g salt, 7.5g fiber, 50g carbs, 7g protein

A healthy variation on a classic crisp. Look for ripe plums because they are naturally sweet.

INGREDIENTS

8 ripe red plums, pitted and quartered
¼ cup low-fat spread
3 tablespoons raw brown sugar
1 tablespoon light corn syrup
1¼ cups rolled oats
½ cup whole-wheat flour

1. Preheat the oven to 350°F. Arrange the plums in a 1-quart baking dish.

2. Put the spread, sugar, and syrup in a small saucepan over low heat. Heat gently, stirring, until the spread is just melted. Remove from the heat and stir in the oats and flour, mixing evenly.

3. Spread the crisp mixture evenly over the plums. Bake in the preheated oven for 20–25 minutes, or until the topping is golden brown and the plums are tender. Serve hot or cold.

1
2
3

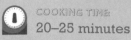

GOES WELL WITH
Serve with a spoonful
of low-fat crème
fraîche or Greek yogurt.

Roasted Vegetables

SERVES 4

PREP TIME:
15 minutes

COOKING TIME:
35–40 minutes

nutritional information per serving	91 cal, 2.5g fat, 0.5g sat fat, 11g total sugars, trace salt, 6g fiber, 14g carbs, 3g protein

A bright and colorful dish that is crammed with fiber and beneficial plant chemicals.

INGREDIENTS

1 onion, cut into wedges

2–4 garlic cloves, with skins

1 small eggplant, trimmed and cut into cubes

1 zucchini, trimmed and cut into chunks

½ butternut squash, peeled, seeded, and cut into small wedges

2 assorted colored bell peppers, seeded and cut into chunks

2 teaspoons olive oil

1 tablespoon shredded fresh basil

pepper, to taste

1. Preheat the oven to 400°F. Put the onion wedges, garlic cloves, and eggplant cubes in a large roasting pan.

2. Add the zucchini, squash, and bell peppers to the roasting pan, then pour over the oil the vegetables. Turn the vegetables until they are lightly coated in the oil.

3. Roast the vegetables for 35–40 minutes, or until softened but not mushy. Turn the vegetables over occasionally during cooking.

4. Remove the vegetables from the oven, season with pepper to taste and stir. Sprinkle with shredded basil and serve immediately. Advise the diners to push the garlic flesh out of the skins.

HEALTHY HINT

Having a variety of colors for the vegetables helps to make sure there is a good range of nutrients.

Fuller for longer

Extra low sat fat

Super low calorie

Raw Beet & Pecan Side Salad

 SERVES 4

PREP TIME:
10 minutes

COOKING TIME:
No cooking

nutritional information per serving	121 cal, 10g fat, 1g sat fat, 5g total sugars, 0.1g salt, 2g fiber, 6g carbs, 1.5g protein

Originally grown just for its leaves, beet is a rich source of folic acid and iron.

INGREDIENTS

2 fresh beets, shredded

8 radishes, thinly sliced

2 scallions, finely chopped

¼ cup coarsely chopped pecans

8 raddichio leaves or crisp lettuce leaves

dressing

2 tablespoons extra virgin olive oil

1 tablespoon balsamic vinegar

2 teaspoons creamed horseradish sauce

salt and pepper, to taste

1. Combine the beet, radishes, scallions, and pecans in a bowl and toss well to mix evenly.

2. Put all the dressing ingredients in a small bowl and whisk lightly with a fork. Season with salt and pepper and pour the dressing over the vegetables in the bowl, tossing to coat evenly.

3. Arrange the raddichio or lettuce leaves on a serving platter and spoon the salad over them.

4. Serve the salad cold on its own or as an accompaniment to main dishes.

1   2   2

SOMETHING DIFFERENT

Wrap the salad in larger lettuce leaves, such as romaine, to make packages for picnics that are easier to transport.

Fuller for longer

Extra low sat fat

Super low calorie

Mixed Cabbage Coleslaw

 SERVES 4

PREP TIME:
10–15 minutes

COOKING TIME:
No cooking

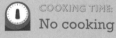

nutritional information per serving	132 cal, 0.9g fat, 0.2g sat fat, 26g total sugars, 0.2g salt, 7g fiber, 28g carbs, 3.5g protein

This slaw is ideal with cold chicken or ham and is high in crunch and vitamin C.

INGREDIENTS

¼ head of red cabbage

⅛ head green cabbage

¼ head of Chinese white cabbage or additional green cabbage

3 carrots, shredded

1 onion, finely sliced

2 Gala or Red Delicious apples, cored and chopped

¼ cup orange juice

2 celery stalks, finely sliced

⅓ cup canned corn kernels

2 tablespoons raisins

dressing

¼ cup low-fat plain yogurt

1 tablespoon chopped fresh flat-leaf parsley

pepper, to taste

1. Discard the outer leaves and hard central core from the cabbages and shred finely. Wash well in plenty of cold water and drain thoroughly.

2. Put the cabbages in a bowl and stir in the carrots and onion. Toss the apples in the orange juice and add to the cabbages together with any remaining orange juice, and the celery, corn, and raisins. Mix well.

3. For the dressing, put the yogurt and parsley in a bowl, season with pepper, and mix well, then pour the dressing over the vegetables. Stir and serve.

Fuller for longer

Extra low sat fat

Spicy Bok Choy with Sesame Sauce

SERVES 4

PREP TIME: 10 minutes

COOKING TIME: 10–15 minutes

nutritional information per serving	163 cal, 14g fat, 2g sat fat, 4.5g total sugars, 1.7g salt, 3.5g fiber, 4.5g carbs, 4.5g protein

Many of us find leafy greens boring. Well, try this flavor-packed dish—it will change your mind.

INGREDIENTS

2 teaspoons peanut oil or vegetable oil

1 red chile, seeded and thinly sliced

1 garlic clove, thinly sliced

5 small bok choys, quartered

½ cup vegetable stock

sauce

2½ tablespoons sesame seeds

2 tablespoons dark soy sauce

2 teaspoons packed light brown sugar

1 garlic clove, crushed

3 tablespoons sesame oil

1. For the sesame sauce, toast the sesame seeds in a dry skillet set over medium heat, stirring until lightly browned. Remove from the heat and cool slightly. Transfer to a mortar and pestle. Add the soy sauce, sugar, and crushed garlic and pound to a coarse paste. Stir in the sesame oil.

2. Heat the peanut oil in a wok or large skillet. Add the chile and sliced garlic and stir-fry for 20–30 seconds. Add the bok choy and stir-fry for 5 minutes, adding the stock a little at a time to prevent sticking.

3. Transfer the bok choy to a warm dish, drizzle the sesame sauce over the top, and serve immediately.

1

2

2

GOES WELL WITH
This bok choy tastes great with plain broiled or teriyaki salmon, or stir-fried lean beef or pork strips.

Low on carbs

Fuller for longer

Extra low sat fat

Almond Green Beans

 SERVES 4

PREP TIME:
5 minutes

COOKING TIME:
5–8 minutes

nutritional information per serving	156 cal, 14g fat, 2.5g sat fat, 2.5g total sugars, 0.1g salt, 2.2g fiber, 3g carbs, 4.5g protein

Almonds and beans are a heavenly, healthy combination, and perfect with almost any kind of meat or fish.

INGREDIENTS

3 cups trimmed green beans

1 tablespoon sunflower oil

½ cup slivered almonds

2 tablespoons low-fat spread

2 teaspoons lemon juice

2 tablespoons finely chopped fresh flat-leaf parsley

salt and pepper, to taste

1. Bring a saucepan of lightly salted water to a boil. Add the beans, bring back to a boil, and boil for 3–5 minutes, or until tender. Drain well.

2. Meanwhile, heat the oil in a large skillet over high heat. Add the almonds and cook, stirring, until golden brown, being careful that they do not burn. Set aside. Use a slotted spoon to transfer the almonds to to a plate lined with paper towels and drain well. Wipe out the skillet.

3. Melt the spread in the skillet. Add the beans and stir. Add the lemon juice and season with salt and pepper then stir in the parsley. Transfer the beans to a serving dish and sprinkle with the almonds to serve.

1

2

3

Hot & Sour Zucchini

 SERVES 4

 PREP TIME:
30 minutes

 COOKING TIME:
5 minutes

nutritional information per serving	86 cal, 7g fat, 1.4g sat fat, 4g total sugars, 1.9g salt, 1.1g fiber, 4g carbs, 1.7g protein

In a traditional Chinese style, this is just one more way to serve the humble zucchini.

INGREDIENTS

2 large zucchini, thinly sliced

1 teaspoon salt

2 tablespoons peanut oil

1 teaspoon Sichuan peppercorns, crushed

½ –1 red chile, seeded and sliced into thin strips

1 large garlic clove, thinly sliced

½ teaspoon minced fresh ginger

1 tablespoon rice vinegar

1 tablespoon light soy sauce

2 teaspoons sugar

1 scallion, green part included, thinly sliced

a few drops of sesame oil and 1 teaspoon sesame seeds, to garnish

1. Put the zucchini slices in a large colander and toss with the salt. Cover with a plate and put a weight on top. Let drain for 20 minutes. Rinse off the salt and spread out the slices on paper towels to dry.

2. Preheat a wok over high heat and add the peanut oil. Add the Sichuan peppercorns, chile, garlic, and ginger. Sauté for about 20 seconds, until the garlic is just beginning to color.

3. Add the zucchini slices and toss in the oil. Add the rice vinegar, soy sauce, and sugar, and stir-fry for 2 minutes. Add the scallion and sauté for 30 seconds. Garnish with the sesame oil and seeds, and serve immediately.

1

2

3

COOK'S NOTE

Don't skip on salting the zucchini—it helps to draw out the excess water that can make the dish soggy.

Fuller for longer

Extra low sat fat

Super low calorie

Sweet & Sour Red Cabbage

 SERVES 6

PREP TIME:
10 minutes

COOKING TIME:
15–20 minutes

nutritional information per serving	102 cal, 3g fat, 0.5g sat fat, 16.3g total sugars, trace salt, 4.5g fiber, 17g carbs, 1.5g protein

We've boosted the flavor and reduced the fat in this dish, which is a great accompaniment to lean pork.

INGREDIENTS

1 head of red cabbage

2 tablespoons olive oil

2 onions, finely sliced

1 garlic clove, chopped

2 small Granny Smith apples, peeled, cored, and sliced

2 tablespoons brown sugar

½ teaspoon ground cinnamon

1 teaspoon crushed juniper berries

whole nutmeg, for grating

2 tablespoons red wine vinegar

grated rind and juice of 1 orange

2 tablespoons red currant jelly or grape jelly

salt and pepper, to taste

1. Cut the cabbage into quarters, remove the central core, and finely shred the leaves.

2. Heat the oil in a large saucepan over medium heat and add the cabbage, onions, garlic, and apples. Stir in the sugar, cinnamon, and juniper berries and grate a quarter of the nutmeg into the pan.

3. Pour in the vinegar and orange juice and add the orange rind.

4. Stir well and season with salt and pepper. The pan will be full, but the volume of the cabbage will reduce during cooking.

5. Cook over medium heat, stirring occasionally, until the cabbage is just tender but still is firm to the bite. This will take 10–15 minutes, depending on how finely the cabbage is sliced.

6. Stir in the red currant jelly, then taste and adjust the seasoning, adding salt and pepper, if necessary. Serve immediately.

2

3

6

BE PREPARED
You can make
this in advance
and store it in
a lidded container
in the refrigerator
for up to a day
before serving.

Low on carbs

Fuller for longer

Extra low sat fat

Super low calorie

Shrimp Wonton Baskets

SERVES 4

PREP TIME:
10 minutes

COOKING TIME:
4–5 minutes

nutritional information per serving	146 cal, 9g fat, 1.5g sat fat, 1g total sugars, 0.9g salt, 2g fiber, 8g carbs, 8g protein

These crunchy little cups are great for a snack or a party canapé that won't break your diet.

INGREDIENTS

sesame oil, for greasing and brushing
12 wonton wrappers
1 ripe avocado
1 tablespoon lime juice
6 ounces cooked, peeled shrimp
1 tablespoon snipped fresh chives
1 teaspoon soy sauce
pepper, to taste
sesame seeds, to serve

1. Preheat the oven to 400°F. Grease 12 cups in a muffin pan.

2. Press wonton wrappers into the prepared cups in the pan, then brush with sesame oil. Bake in the preheated oven for 4–5 minutes, or until crisp and golden. Let cool on a wire rack.

3. Meanwhile, halve the avocado, remove the pit, and scoop out the flesh. Cut into small dice, sprinkle with lime juice, and mix with the shrimp and chives in a bowl. Season with pepper.

4. Spoon the avocado mixture into the wonton cups and splash the tops with soy sauce. Sprinkle with sesame seeds just before serving.

BE PREPARED
If you are making these for a party, prepare to the end of step 3 earlier in the day, chill the filling, and assemble before serving.

Fuller for longer

Extra low sat fat

Wheat, gluten
& dairy free

Spiced Basmati Rice

 SERVES 4

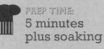 PREP TIME:
5 minutes
plus soaking

COOKING TIME:
15–20 minutes

nutritional information per serving	260 cal, 6.5g fat, 3g sat fat, 0g total sugars, 1.5g salt, trace fiber, 42g carbs, 4g protein

Basmati rice has a lower glycemic index than other types of carb, and this dish is packed with flavor, too.

INGREDIENTS

1¼ cups basmati rice or other long-grain rice

2 tablespoons vegetable oil or peanut oil

5 green cardamom pods, bruised

5 cloves

½ cinnamon stick

1 teaspoon fennel seeds

½ teaspoon black mustard seeds

2 bay leaves

2 cups water

1½ teaspoons salt, or to taste

pepper, to taste

1. Rinse the rice in several changes of water until the water runs clear, then let soak for 30 minutes. Drain and set aside until ready to cook.

2. Heat a large saucepan with a tight-fitting lid over medium–high heat, then add the oil. Add the spices and bay leaves and stir for 30 seconds. Stir the rice into the pan so the grains are coated with oil. Stir in the water and salt and bring to a boil.

3. Reduce the heat to as low as possible and cover the pan tightly. Simmer, without lifting the lid, for 8–10 minutes, or according to the package directions, until the grains are tender and all the liquid has been absorbed.

4. Turn off the heat and use two forks to mix in the rice. Season to taste with pepper. Replace the lid on the pan and let stand for 5 minutes before serving.

1

2

4

HEALTHY HINT
Peanut oil is higher in healthier types of fat than other oils, so use it if you can find it.

Mexican Rice

 SERVES 4

PREP TIME:
10 minutes

COOKING TIME:
20–25 minutes

nutritional information
per serving

209 cal, 0.7g fat, 0.1g sat fat, 4g total sugars, trace salt,
2g fiber, 42g carbs, 5g protein

*A simple and tasty low-fat rice dish that makes
a great accompaniment for broiled chicken.*

INGREDIENTS

1 onion, chopped

6 plum tomatoes, peeled,
seeded, and chopped

1 cup vegetable stock

1 cup long-grain rice

salt and pepper, to taste

1. Put the onion and tomatoes in a food processor and process to a smooth puree. Scrape the puree into a saucepan, pour in the stock, and bring to a boil over medium heat, stirring occasionally.

2. Add the rice and stir once, then reduce the heat, cover, and simmer for 20–25 minutes, or until all the liquid has been absorbed and the rice is tender. Season with salt and pepper and serve immediately.

SOMETHING
DIFFERENT
Spice up this
Mexican rice
dish by adding
some chopped
fresh chiles,
garlic, and
cilantro at the
start of step 2.

Fuller for longer

Extra low sat fat

Peanut Dip with Pita Chips

 SERVES 6

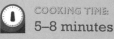 PREP TIME:
5 minutes

COOKING TIME:
5–8 minutes

nutritional information per serving	280 cal, 17g fat, 3g sat fat, 2.5g total sugars, 1g salt, 3g fiber, 21g carbs, 10g protein

Rich in protein, peanut butter is a useful pantry standby for easy snacks.

INGREDIENTS

⅔ cup chunky peanut butter

1 small red chile, seeded and finely chopped

2 teaspoons dark soy sauce

juice of 1 lime

3–4 tablespoons water

4 small pita breads

sesame oil, for spraying

1 tablespoon sesame seeds

salt and pepper, to taste

1. Put the peanut butter, chile, soy sauce, and lime juice in a saucepan over low heat. Cook gently without boiling, stirring, until evenly mixed. Stir in just enough water to make a soft paste. Season with salt and pepper. Set aside and keep warm.

2. Preheat a broiler to high. Slice the pita breads into strips about ¾ inch wide and arrange in a single layer on a baking sheet. Spray lightly with sesame oil and sprinkle with the sesame seeds.

3. Broil the pitas for 2–3 minutes, turning once, until golden and crisp.

4. Spoon the peanut dip into a small bowl and serve warm, with the pita chips on the side for dipping.

1   1   2

HEALTHY HINT
For an extra healthy snack, replace the pita breads with raw vegetable crudités, such as sticks of carrot and celery.

Sweet Potato Fries

Fuller for longer

Extra low sat fat

Wheat, gluten
& dairy free

 SERVES 4

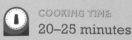 PREP TIME:
10 minutes

COOKING TIME:
20–25 minutes

nutritional information per serving	202 cal, 1.5g fat, 0.5g sat fat, 12g total sugars, 0.7g salt, 7g fiber, 48g carbs, 3g protein

You'll absolutely love these low-fat, vitamin-C rich sweet potato chips as a change from potato chips.

INGREDIENTS

2 sprays vegetable oil spray
4 large sweet potatoes
½ teaspoon salt
½ teaspoon ground cumin
¼ teaspoon cayenne pepper

1. Preheat the oven to 375°F. Spray a large baking sheet with vegetable oil spray.

2. Peel the sweet potatoes and slice into ¼-inch thick spears about 3 inches long. Spread the sweet potatoes on the prepared baking sheet and spray them with vegetable oil spray.

3. In a small bowl, combine the salt, cumin, and cayenne. Sprinkle the spice mixture evenly over the sweet potatoes and then toss to coat.

4. Spread the sweet potatoes out into a single layer and bake in the preheated oven for about 20–25 minutes, or until cooked through and lightly colored. Serve hot.

SOMETHING DIFFERENT

Instead of the salt, cumin, and cayenne, you can use 1¼ teaspoons Cajun seasoning.

Eggplant Pâté

🍴 SERVES 6   👨‍🍳 PREP TIME: 10 minutes plus cooling   ⏱ COOKING TIME: 1¼ hours

nutritional information per serving	73 cal, 7.5g fat, 1g sat fat, 1g total sugars, trace salt, 1.3g fiber, 8g carbs, 1.4g protein

This is also known as "poor man's caviar" because the humble eggplant tastes so delicious in this recipe.

INGREDIENTS

2 large eggplants
¼ cup extra virgin olive oil
2 garlic cloves, minced
¼ cup lemon juice
salt and pepper, to taste
2 tablespoons coarsely chopped
fresh flat-leaf parsley, to garnish
6 crisp breads, to serve

1. Preheat the oven to 350°F. Score the skins of the eggplants with the tip of a sharp knife, without piercing the flesh, and put them on a baking sheet. Bake for 1¼ hours, or until soft.

2. Remove the eggplants from the oven and let sit until cool enough to handle. Cut them in half and, using a spoon, scoop out the flesh into a bowl. Mash the flesh thoroughly.

3. Gradually beat in the olive oil, then stir in the garlic and lemon juice. Season with salt and pepper. Cover with plastic wrap and store in the refrigerator until required. Sprinkle with the parsley and serve with crisp breads.

1   2   3

COOK'S NOTE
This makes a great dip, too, served with sticks of carrot, celery, and bell pepper.

Marshmallow & Cranberry Mini Muffins

 MAKES 48   PREP TIME: 10 minutes   COOKING TIME: 12–15 minutes

nutritional information per muffin	38 cal, 1g fat, 0.1g sat fat, 2g total sugars, 0.1g salt, 0.3g fiber, 6g carbs, 0.7g protein

These tasty little low-fat muffins are bite-size, so they are just enough to satisfy sweet cravings.

INGREDIENTS

1⅔ cups all-purpose flour

1 tablespoon baking powder

⅓ cup firmly packed light brown sugar

¾ cup dried cranberries

½ cup miniature marshmallows

finely grated rind of ½ small lemon

1 tablespoon lemon juice

1 egg, beaten

½ cup skim milk

3 tablespoons sunflower oil

½ teaspoon vanilla extract

1. Preheat the oven to 400°F. Put 48 paper cupcake liners on two or three baking sheets or in cupcake pans.

2. Sift the flour and baking powder into a bowl and add the sugar. Stir in the cranberries and marshmallows.

3. Whisk together lemon rind and juice, egg, milk, oil, and vanilla in a bowl, then stir into the dry ingredients to make a soft batter.

4. Spoon the batter into the paper liners and bake in the preheated oven for 12–15 minutes, or until risen, firm, and golden. Transfer to a wire rack to cool before serving.

2   3   4

COOK'S NOTE

If you are using paper muffin cups, it helps to use a double layer of cups so the muffins keep a better shape.

Caramel Popcorn Bites

 SERVES 8

 PREP TIME:
1¼ hours

COOKING TIME:
5 minutes

nutritional information per serving	230 cal, 7.5g fat, 2.5g sat fat, 38g total sugars, 1.3g salt, trace fiber, 44g carbs, 0.7g protein

Popcorn is one of the lowest calorie snacks you can choose, and our quick recipe is really special.

INGREDIENTS

½ cup granulated sugar

½ cup firmly packed light brown sugar

½ cup light corn syrup

2 tablespoons butter

1½ teaspoon baking soda

1 teaspoon salt

½ teaspoon vanilla extract

10 cups plain, air-popped popcorn

1. Cover a large baking sheet with parchment paper or aluminum foil.

2. In a saucepan, combine the sugars, light corn syrup, and butter and bring to a boil over medium–high heat. Reduce the heat to medium and boil, without stirring, for 4 minutes. Carefully stir in the baking soda, salt, and vanilla extract.

3. Put the popcorn in a large mixing bowl. Pour the caramel over the popcorn and stir to coat. Using two spoons, form the mixture into 24 balls, about 2 inches in diameter, and place them on the lined baking sheet. Let sit at room temperature for about 1 hour or until firm. Serve at room temperature.

2

3

3

Fuller for longer

Extra low sat fat

Super low calorie

Apple Dips

 SERVES 4

 PREP TIME:
10 minutes
plus cooling

COOKING TIME:
10 minutes

nutritional information per serving	106 cal, 0.5g fat, 0.2g sat fat, 23g total sugars, trace salt, 4g fiber, 24g carbs, 2.4g protein

A high fiber, low glycemic index snack with no added sugar, so they are good for a lunch-box surprise.

INGREDIENTS

4 Gala, Fuji, or other sweet apples

finely grated rind and juice of 1 orange

⅔ cup low-fat plain yogurt

1. Thinly peel, core, and coarsely chop two of the apples and put in a saucepan with the orange rind and about two-thirds of the juice over low heat. Heat gently until boiling, then cover and simmer gently, stirring occasionally, for 6–8 minutes, to soften.

2. Remove from the heat and process with an electric handheld immersion blender or in a food processor until smooth. Let cool completely.

3. Core the remaining two apples and cut into thick slices. Toss the slices in the remaining orange juice to prevent them from browning.

4. Stir the yogurt lightly into the applesauce in a small bowl. Serve in small dish or bowls, with the apple slices on the side for dipping.

HEALTHY HINT
For a dairy-free version, you can omit the yogurt or simply replace it with soy yogurt.

Beet Brownie Bites

 MAKES 36

PREP TIME:
25 minutes

COOKING TIME:
25–30 minutes

nutritional information per bite	75 cal, 4g fat, 1.5g sat fat, 7g total sugars, trace salt, 0.5g fiber, 10g carbs, 1.5g protein

Dark chocolate and beet are rich in antioxidants, so these gooey treats are not as wicked as they look.

INGREDIENTS

6 ounces semisweet chocolate, broken into small pieces

2 eggs

1 teaspoon vanilla extract

⅔ cup firmly packed dark brown sugar

⅓ cup sunflower oil, plus extra for greasing

4 cooked beets, grated

¾ cup all-purpose flour

¾ teaspoon baking powder

3 tablespoons unsweetened cocoa powder

1. Preheat the oven to 350°F. Lightly grease an 8-inch square baking pan and line with parchment paper.

2. Put the chocolate in a heatproof bowl, set over a saucepan of gently simmering water, and heat until just melted. Remove from the heat.

3. Put the eggs, vanilla, and sugar in a bowl and beat at high speed with an electric mixer for 3–4 minutes, or until pale and frothy. Beat in the oil. Stir in the beet, then sift in the flour, baking powder, and cocoa and fold in. Add the melted chocolate and stir evenly.

4. Spoon the batter into the prepared pan and bake in the preheated oven for 25–30 minutes, or until just firm to the touch. Let cool in the pan, then turn out and let cool completely on a wire rack.

5. Cut into about 36 bite-size squares and serve.

FREEZING TIP
Pack the brownies into an airtight freezer container, seal, label, and freeze for up to three months. Thaw at room temperature.

Lemon Meringue Cookies

SERVES 8

PREP TIME:
10 minutes

COOKING TIME:
2 hours

nutritional information per serving	73 cal, 0g fat, 0g sat fat, 17g total sugars, 0.3g salt, 0g fiber, 18g carbs, 0.7g protein

A fat-free, low-calorie treat, ideal for a mid-afternoon break with a hot drink.

INGREDIENTS

2 extra-large egg whites
⅛ teaspoon cream of tartar
pinch of salt
¾ cup granulated sugar
finely grated zest of 1 lemon

1. Preheat the oven to 225°F. Line a large baking sheet with aluminum foil or parchment paper.

2. In a large, grease-free bowl, beat the egg whites with an electric mixer on high speed until they are frothy. Add the cream of tartar and salt and continue to beat on high until soft peaks form. Gradually add the sugar and continue to beat on high for about 3–4 minutes, or until stiff peaks form. Fold in the lemon zest.

3. Drop the batter in rounded teaspoons onto the prepared baking sheet. Bake in the preheated oven for about 1½ hours, or until dry and crisp but not yet beginning to color. Turn off the oven and let the cookies sit inside the oven for an additional 30 minutes. Serve at room temperature.

2

2

3

BE PREPARED
Meringues store well in an airtight container for several weeks or more—so make them in advance for unexpected guests.

Extra low sat fat

Maple-Nut Granola Bars

 MAKES 12

 PREP TIME:
15 minutes
plus chilling

COOKING TIME:
5–7 minutes

nutritional information per bar	200 cal, 10g fat, 1.5g sat fat, 11g total sugars, 0.2g salt, 2g fiber, 22.8g carbs, 5g protein

These granola bars have all the flavor of a oat bar, but are packed with healthy nuts and seeds.

INGREDIENTS

1 spray vegetable oil spray

1¾ cups rolled oats

½ cup chopped pecans

½ cup slivered almonds

½ cup maple syrup

¼ cup firmly packed light brown sugar

¼ cup smooth peanut butter

1 teaspoon vanilla extract

¼ teaspoon salt

2 cups puffed rice cereal

¼ cup ground flaxseed

1. Preheat the oven to 350°F. Coat a 9 x 13-inch baking pan with vegetable oil spray.

2. On a separate large, rimmed baking sheet, combine the oats, pecans, and almonds and toast in the preheated oven for 5–7 minutes, or until lightly browned.

3. Meanwhile, combine the maple syrup, brown sugar, and peanut butter in a small saucepan and bring to a boil over medium heat. Cook, stirring, for about 4–5 minutes, or until the mixture thickens slightly. Stir in vanilla extract and salt.

4. When the oats and nuts are toasted, put them in a mixing bowl and add the rice cereal and flaxseed. Add the syrup mixture to the oat mixture and stir to combine. Spread the syrup-oat mixture into the prepared baking pan and chill for at least 1 hour before cutting into 12 bars. Store in a tightly covered container at room temperature. Serve at room temperature.

HEALTHY HINT
For a more fruity option, try replacing half of the sugar in this recipe with the same weight of finely chopped dried apricots.

Fuller for longer

Extra low sat fat

Healthy Hot Chocolate

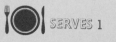 SERVES 1

PREP TIME:
5 minutes

COOKING TIME:
5 minutes

nutritional information per serving	260 cal, 4g fat, 2g sat fat, 29g total sugars, 0.9g salt, 5g fiber, 48g carbs, 12g protein

Cocoa can help lower blood pressure and improve cholesterol levels while skim milk is calcium rich.

INGREDIENTS

1 tablespoon sugar

2 tablespoons unsweetened cocoa powder

pinch of ground cinnamon (optional)

1 cup skim milk

¼ teaspoon vanilla extract

1 large marshmallow

1. In a small saucepan, combine the sugar, cocoa powder, cinnamon, if using, and about 2 tablespoons of the milk. Stir to make a paste.

2. Add the remaining milk and heat to a simmer over medium heat. Cook, stirring occasionally, for about 3 minutes, until the cocoa and sugar are completely dissolved.

3. Stir in vanilla extract and serve immediately, topped with a marshmallow.

SOMETHING
DIFFERENT
For a special winter
treat, add a sprinkling
of nutmeg over the top
of the hot chocolate.

Skinny Strawberry Fizz Cocktail

 SERVES 4

PREP TIME:
10 minutes

COOKING TIME:
No cooking

nutritional information per serving	93 cal, 0g fat, 0g sat fat, 8.5g total sugars, trace salt, 0.8g fiber, 9g carbs, 0.5g protein

Cocktails can be high in calories, but this one will let you have the occasional guilt-free tipple.

INGREDIENTS

8 ounces strawberries, hulled

2 tablespoons agave syrup

juice of 1 lime

½ cup crushed ice

½ cup vodka

1¾ cups diet cola

whole strawberries and strips of lime zest, to decorate

1. Put the strawberries, syrup, and lime in a plastic pitcher and process with an electric handheld immersion blender or in a food processor until smooth.

2. Add 2 tablespoons of crushed ice to each of four tall glasses.

3. Pour the strawberry mixture evenly into each glass, add 2 tablespoons of vodka to each glass, and stir to mix.

4. Fill up the glasses with the cola to taste, place a strawberry and strips of lime zest on the rims, and serve immediately.

HEALTHY HINT
For an alcohol-free version with even less calories, you can simply omit the vodka and serve as a delicious mocktail.